Wilton's Wit

A Collection of Essays

From a Life of Service

In the Ministry of

Jesus Christ

Clyde C. Wilton

Order this book online at www.trafford.com
or email orders@trafford.com

Most Trafford titles are also available at major online book retailers.

Printed in the United States of America.

ISBN: 978-1-4269-3383-7 (soft)

*Our mission is to efficiently provide the world's finest, most comprehensive book publishing
service, enabling every author to experience success. To find out how to publish your book, your
way, and have it available worldwide, visit us online at www.trafford.com*

Trafford rev. 7/27/2010

 www.trafford.com

North America & international
toll-free: 1 888 232 4444 (USA & Canada)
phone: 250 383 6864 ♦ fax: 812 355 4082

Preface

We are living in a day of electronic technology. We think that we must have instant communication and that we must have a cell phone to carry with us at all times. Yes, we are hooked up with the world. We can bring the World Series into our living rooms, along with a daily review of earthquakes, hurricanes, wars, and spectacular happenings worldwide. This is a different world from the one I grew up in.

My world was a small farm in North Texas. Our communication system was a telephone about the size of a small suitcase nailed to the wall and operated by two "B" batteries about the size of medium-sized pickle jars.

We were hooked up with Grandpa about a half mile to the West, and for awhile, we were hooked up to a party line that went all the way to Uncle Jake about 3 miles to the East. The radio was just coming in when I was a boy. I learned to make crystal set radios that consisted of a little wire called a "Cat Tail," a crystal about the size of a small marble, copper wire wrapped around a coil about the size of a hot dog, and some headphones. I remember getting really excited when I got a signal from Chicago, and one time I got a signal all the way from Mexico!   I started school at age 7 in the one room, one teacher schoolhouse that I walked to each day.

I remember The Depression well. Since we lived on a farm, we had lots of good vegetables from the garden, plenty of eggs from the chicken hens, and milk from the cows. Occasionally in the wintertime we killed a hog for meat.

We composed songs that visualized the situation. I still remember a part of one song: "Eleven cent cotton and 40 cent meat, how in the world can a poor man eat? Flour up high and cotton down low, how in the world can we raise the dough?" It was simple world, and I am grateful to have been a part of it. I am also grateful to have been catapulted into this world of technology.

The Lord has given me so many interesting things to do and to see that I want to share them. It has been my privilege to travel around the world. I went to a crusade in India one time. Going, I took the Pacific route, and coming home, the Atlantic route. A sight to behold, was seeing the Sphinx to my right and the city of Cairo to my left from the top of a great pyramid in Egypt!

Experiences from my life are in essay from in my book, Wilton's Wit. It goes back to a buggy ride with my mother and grandmother and to school days and the influence of some of my good teachers. Several essays were written when I was a chaplain in the Air Force. So, some of the essays were written many years ago, and some were written recently.

The Lord called me into the Ministry of Preaching the Gospel of Christ in 1940. Along with preaching is loving the people and trying to encourage them along the way. Wilton's Wit is an attempt to extend my ministry. If these essays are a blessing to you then I will have accomplished what I wanted to do.

"Blessings to you," is my prayer.

For my wife, LaRue, you live on in my heart, as beautiful as the day I met you.

The pictures sprinkled throughout the text are pictures of the people and places I remember fondly and the inspiration for mot of my essays. Thank you to Verda Lee Crum King for her pictures of her family farm in the Winn Hill Community where I grew up.

This book was prepared with the assistance of my good friend, Maryanne Rivers, and my son, Aaron Wilton. I thank them for their hard work and thoughtful suggestions.

Table Of Contents

#	Title	Page
1	A Point Of View	13-14
2	A Red-Letter Day	15-17
3	A Trip To Remember	18-19
4	Time	20-21
5	Unconscious Influence	22-23
6	Thoughts—The Making Of Man	24-25
7	The Moment Of Truth	26-27
8	Thank You	28-29
9	Miss Edna	30-31
10	Lost Without Knowing It	32-33
11	Limited Knowledge	34-35
12	Help	36-37
13	Grandpa's Advice	38-39
14	Grandpa's Experience	40-41
15	Christmas 2001	42-43
16	Changing The Price Tags	44-45
17	The Fast Time Period	46-47
18	Ancient Code Provides Rules For Today's Life	48-49
19	Conquer Tensions By Devine Rejuvenation	50-51
20	Sacrifices And Conveniences	52-53
21	'Best Seller' Authored By 44 Over 2000 Years	54-55
22	Christianity Provides Moral Law Foundation	56-57
23	Abundant Living Through Spiritual Maturity	58-59
24	Art Of Helping Others Brings Vast Dividends	60-61
25	Happiness: The Key Could Be In The Present, Not The Future	62-63
26	A Quality Thought Process, A Key to Quality Life	64-65

#	Title	Page
27	Easter Points To Time For Spiritual Growth	66-67
28	Marital Problems	68-70
29	Military Service Seen As A Test Of Character	71-72
30	Peace For Individual, World Starts With Self	73-74
31	Personal Security Is Based On Trust In God	75-76
32	Early Start In Setting Spiritual Example Cited	77-78
33	Example Of Parent In Both Word And Deed Cited	79-80
34	Spiritual Power Seen As Top Dynamic Force	81-82
35	Space Age Invokes New Concept Of Stewardship	83-84
36	Opportunities	85-86
37	Good Food	87-88
38	Count Your Blessings On Thanksgiving Day	89-90
39	Opportunity for More Abundant Life Is Ours	91
40	Man Breaks Man's Laws; God's Are Unbreakable	92-93
41	Easter Message Is Same Today As Centuries Ago	94-95
42	Joy Of Worship Makes Life Sweet, Wonderful	96-97
43	The Key To Peace Is Within Everyone	98
44	Inventory Of Personal Life Leads To Victory	99-100
45	Aesop's Fables Still Contain Valuable Lessons For Today	101-102
46	Self Evaluation Is Key To Well-Balanced Life	103-104

#	*Title*	*Page*
47	Many Prefer Being A Religious Spectator	105-106
48	Watch Those Thoughts	107-108
49	Past Experiences Should Help In Building For Future	109-110
50	Man Must Prepare For Eternal Career Today	111-112
51	Man's Search For God Seen In All Of History	113-114
52	Living A Godly Life Calls For Godly Reasoning	115-116
53	Opportunity Seen With Growth In Grace Of God	117-118
54	Power Of Good Thought Determines Character	119-120
55	Prayer Gives Feeling Of Deep Understanding	121-122
56	Spiritual 'Suicide' Is Danger To Many Others	123-124
57	Weapon To Stop Spread Of Communism And Terrorism Is Basic	125-127
58	Seeking For The Chief Good	128-129
59	My Dad's Razor Strap	130-131
60	Daily Fellowship With God Solves Problems	132-133
61	Atmosphere Of Church Seen As 'Penetrating'	134
62	Attending Church Vital To Sincere Churchgoer	135-136
63	Brotherhood's Concept Is Key To World Peace	137-138
64	Gift Of Love Praised By Paul As Best of All	139
65	Heavenly Rewards Come From the Wise Use of Time	140-141
66	The Memory Bank	142-143

#	Title	Page
67	Only Through Prayer	144-145
68	Communication	146-147
69	The Honey Bee	148-150
70	My Church	151-153
71	Stewart Albert Newman	154-156
72	Complaining	157-158
73	Who Is The Greatest?	159-160
74	It Is Time To Forgive	161-162
75	Casual Learning	163-164
76	Grandpa Rhoades	165-166
77	The Need For Friends	167-169
78	Is Your Church A Building	170-171
79	From A Worm To A Butterfly	172-173
80	The Voice Of God	174-175
81	Jermyn High School	176-178
82	The Trip To Alaska	179-182
83	A Week In Thorne Bay, Alaska	183-185
84	Guyana, South America	186-188
85	What Is So Wrong About Gambling?	189-190
86	God Told Me So	191-192
87	Why Me Lord?	193-194
88	LaRue Vivian Haley	195-197
89	The Buggy Ride	198-199
90	The Hatchery In Ketchikan: The Salmon Capital Of The World	200-201
91	The Misawa Mission Of The Tokyo Baptist Church	202-203
92	Misawa, Japan	204-208
93	India	209-212
94	Emmanuel Lighthouse Mission	213-215
95	The Garden	216-217

A Point Of View

Where are you today? You are not where you were yesterday and you are not where you will be tomorrow. Yesterday is history and tomorrow is a mystery, so we only live in the present. And today is a wonderful present for us! We will never get to live it again so we need to take it very seriously as it goes by. We may want to go back "to the good old days" or fast-forward to fantasy days in the future, but it does not happen that way. Time is regulated by the Creator, who set it in motion, and we cannot slow it down or speed it up.

We all look at life from different perspectives. Our age, health, education, geographical location, racial extraction, political persuasions, and religious commitments can color how we perceive things. We can liken our journey through life as one with travels through the valleys, the plains, and the mountains; and, as the traveler moves on, the scenery changes.

One day, I had an unusual experience of standing on the Great Pyramid of Giza, one of the Seven Wonders of the Ancient World. To my right I marveled at the inscrutable Sphinx, with a lion's body and a human face, and to my left was the Nile River and the city of Cairo. And standing with me was Father Kinney, a Catholic priest, and our guide, who was a Moslem. We were in unity that day because our objective was to climb the pyramid and see the world  from that point of view. But no doubt we had differences of opinion on theological and political issues.

We start out with a clean slate. Our point of view on the world is rather limited, but if we do not get what we are looking for, we let the world know by crying. When we start to school, we are introduced into a new world of knowledge that makes an indelible impression on our thinking. When we become teenagers, we have matured so much that we now realize how outdated our parents are. And then comes the time that we seek to change the world about us. After we have married and have children, we discover that it is time to go to work and make provisions for the family. In the prime of life, we seek to better ourselves by wearing finer clothes and getting a bigger salary, a faster car, a more luxurious house, and seeking to associate with prestigious people. After that comes the time when we live in the lives of our children, becoming more interested in what they are accomplishing than what we have done. Finally, the sunset years arrive, and we have a time of reflection on many things.

Where do you sit today? What is your point of view? Are you where you want to be? Today, we are the accumulation of all our past experiences. We cannot say what our outlook will be tomorrow. We never know what blessing or tragedy will overtake us. But we can be certain that there will be changes and we need to be prepared to meet them. The Apostle Paul's life was drastically changed one day when he met Jesus on the road to Damascus. He thought that the Christians were a menace to society and they must be destroyed! But after that encounter with Jesus, he became a Christian and completely changed his point of view toward life and reality. Even to the point that he could say, "I have learned that whatever the circumstance is I am self-sufficient." He had been initiated into the grace of God (Cf. Philippians 4: 11-14). We can also stand in God's grace and live victoriously today and be prepared for the mysterious future ahead.

A Red-Letter Day

Life is made up of days. The present is always with us —the past is gone and the future is not here. Henry Ward Beecher said, "Age and youth look upon life from the opposite ends of the telescope: to the one it is exceedingly long, to the other exceedingly short." Of our memories of days gone by, some may bless us, while others may haunt us. Perhaps, some we would like to forget and others we would like to live again. So I assume that we all have some red-letter days that are precious to our memories—maybe a first date, a wedding, a gift, a word of encouragement, a vacation, a graduation, or a trip to an interesting place.

I had one of those red-letter days when I was a young boy, perhaps five or six years old. Many of the 29,715 days of

my life I have forgotten, but that day was one to remember. That day was written indelibly upon the molecules of my brain. It was quality time spent with Pa.

It was a day long ago when our family lived on a small farm in Jack County. We had very little money, so we lived off the land. We raised wheat on the land and then we harvested it, and some of it would be made into flour. There was a grinding mill at Perrin, Texas. So one day, after the wheat had been harvested, Pa let me go with him to get the wheat made into flour. We would go in our big wagon that would hold several bushels of wheat. It was a long trip to Perrin in a wagon. We first had to go east about 12 miles to Jacksboro, and then we turned south for another 16 miles. So that was a round trip of about 60 miles. As well as I can remember, for a successful one-day trip we had to leave our farm before sunup, and we did not get back home until after sundown.

I was excited about making that long trip with Pa. Ma packed us a sack lunch, and we were all set to go early in the morning. I anticipated a great day, just Pa and me. And it was a great day, except for one thing. We had two pet squirrels that we had gotten when they were babies and had fed through a nipple on a milk bottle. They grew up and  were like members of our household. I liked to play with them and really wanted to take them with us on our long trip. I figured Pa wouldn't let me take them, so I didn't ask. Instead, I put one in each of his coat pockets before he put his coat on. My thinking was that once we were down the road, I would show Pa, and everything would be OK. It didn't happen like that, though. A bad thing happened to one of them. Pa didn't know they were stowed away, and when he sat down, he sat on one of them and killed him! I was pretty sad, but I still had one squirrel to play with.

We traveled for hours and it seemed like we would never get there, but finally we did. Many other wagons were there to have their wheat ground into flour, too. Finally, after waiting for some time, we got our wheat ground and made preparation for the trip back home. We had another 30 miles back home in a slow wagon. When we got back, home the sun had set and it was night, but now we had flour so we could have some good biscuits with gravy made from milk from our cows. Pa and I, and one of the squirrels, had made the trip in good shape. The trip was long and tiresome, but, to me, it was quality time spent with Pa, for we had the whole day to ourselves. What a day to remember! Yes, that day was a Red-Letter day, and the memory of it still blesses me.

A Trip To Remember

I still remember a trip that I made with my Dad when I was a small boy — perhaps about 6 or 7 years of age. I have made many other trips since that time, with some taking me even to the other side of the globe, but that trip with my Dad at a very young age was one that shall always be a part of me.

The mode of transportation that day was a big-wheeled farm wagon with a wagon seat in the front that was placed on top of the sides of the bed. The wagon was pulled by two of our workhorses. Perhaps, the most important thing about the trip was that it was planned just for me. I knew that Pa was going to get me a present, but I really was not prepared for the big surprise that it turned out to be. The trip took several hours, but I was so excited that the time passed quickly. We headed out of our farmhouse to the Winn Hill Community and then to Berwick, a community which must have been 6 or

7 miles away. Then we turned north and went to places I had never even heard about. Finally, we came to a big ranch — at least it was big to me!

And then the big surprise...Pa had purchased two little goats just for me! What a thrill that was! It's a thrill even now just thinking of it! We brought them home in the wagon, and as far as I can tell I was the happiest boy in our whole neighborhood...maybe even the happiest boy in Jack County! They were mine to run and jump and play with. I named them Billy and Nanny. They became my cherished playmates. As time passed by, our goat population grew and

Pa fenced off the South Pasture for the goats. Billy and Nanny were always special to me, and they were still with us even when I went off to college.

Yes, that was a trip to remember! Over the years I have traveled by buggy, car, ship, train, plane, but never have I been on a trip that gave me more pleasure and joy than that trip in the wagon on that country dirt road to the goat farm. Pa always did the right things. I always thought he was the greatest person I ever knew. I guess that is why I have always wanted to be that kind of a Pa.

Time

What is Time? It is the system of sequential relations that any event has to any other, whether in the past, present, or future. It is of finite duration, as contrasted with eternity. It is a particular or definite point of time, as indicated by a clock. In one way or another, we all are involved with time.

We use time to measure most everything we do. We are told that light travels at 186,282 miles per second and that the moon, which is 240,000 miles away, takes 27 days to make one revolution. We are also told that a tortoise lives about a 100 years, while some flies live for only one day. We now have some clocks that are so sophisticated that we must add to our vocabulary words that can explain  them. There are stopwatches that can record time to the nearest fifth, tenth, or hundredth of a second, and cameras that can capture fast time to a millisecond — a thousandth of a second — fast enough to create a stop-motion effect. There is also the measurable nanosecond, a billionth of a second, two or four of which are what it takes for a personal computer to  execute a single software command. Today, we have atomic clocks that keep time with such staggering accuracy that they neither lose nor gain more than a second in 3 million years; and, we now have the second defined as exactly 9,192,361,770 cycles of the atomic radiation corresponding to the transition between two electron spin energy levels of the ground state of the cesium 133 atom at 0 K temperature.

So we have come a long way in learning how to measure time. But the practical and personal question is what do with the time we have. Time keeps moving on, and we cannot stop it. Time is precious, and each day is a new gift given to us by the Almighty who created it. Yesterday is gone and tomorrow is not here. So all we have is the present. But if we use the present according to God's plan, we will accumulate memories that will rise up and bless us. Not only that, but each day lived with integrity will prepare us for the new challenges that we will face tomorrow. Nathaniel Hawthorne said, "Time flies over us, but leaves its shadow behind." We often hear people talk about "killing Time!" What a tragedy to kill time—it is too precious to murder. We need to use it wisely. Will Rogers said, "I never yet talked to a man who wanted to save time who could tell me what he was going to do with the time he saved." Today is a blessed gift from God, and it is good if we use it wisely. We can shout in agreement with Ralph Waldo Emerson who said, "This time, like all times, is a very good one, if we but know what to do with it."

Unconscious Influence

There are two kinds of influences in this world. There is conscious influence, which we exert purposely to try to sway another, as by teaching, by argument, by persuasion, by threatening, by gifts, and by promises. And then, there is the other kind of influence which naturally flows out from us by our character and which we may not be consciously aware of.

We are told by some people that character is not important for performing the work that we do. Whether one is a teacher, a plumber, a car salesman, a senator, a lawyer, a doctor or a dentist, or the president of our nation, we are told that if he does his job well, then his personal virtues are of no importance. But what can we say about that unconscious influence that flows out from each individual?

Is this unconscious influence important? Do we think that it is insignificant because it is unnoticed and noiseless? How is it in the natural world? Because they are louder, we may be tempted to think that the frightening noise of the lightning and the blast of thunderstorms which accompany hurricanes and tornadoes may indicate something more powerful than the silent exertion of those tremendous astronomic forces which every moment hold the physical universe together. But without that unseen gravity, we would have no world! This can be applied in the political world. Politicians may make speeches giving all kinds of promises, or even tell us lies which seem right due to their eloquent delivery; but, if they are known to be hypocrites, their words are empty. On the other hand, if the political leader is honest and compassionate, his influence can go far beyond his words.

Is it important for the teacher to have integrity, or is it only important that she or he has important degrees and skill in her or his profession? She may be able to teach reading and mathematics, but if her lifestyle is promiscuous, her influence may be devastating to her students. To learn and apply the multiplication table may be important, but for a life of usefulness it may be more important to learn and apply the Ten Commandments and the golden rule. The same rule can be applied to the lawyer, the doctor, the senator, the car salesman, and even to the President of the USA. Bulwer said, "A good man does good merely by living." So whatever job a person has, it is important to have integrity of character, because what a person is speaks louder than what the spoken words declare. So the influence that is constantly flowing out from you, or me, is inevitable, and it may bless or hurt others without our knowing it. Horace Bushnell said, "If you had the seeds of pestilence in your body you would not have a more active contagion than you have in your tempers, tastes, and principles. Simply to be in the world, whatever you are, is to exert an influence—an influence too, compared with which mere language and persuasion are feeble."

Jesus, the Light of the World, challenges us to be lights that are constantly shining (Matthew 5:14). He is more interested in what a person is, than what a person says. If you do not have that light, he offers it to you now—the light that forever shines to glorify God and to bless others.

Thoughts — The Making Of Man
"Whatsoever a man thinketh in his heart, so is he."
(Proverbs 23:7)

You are not what you think you are, but what you think, you are. You are not what your actions declare you to be. Expediency and pressure from others may cause you to act out of character. You are not what your words say you are. There may be a big gap in what you say and what you really are. You are not what your reputation tells others that you are. You may be better or worse than what other people think of you. You are probably better than what some people think you are, and you are probably worse than what others think you are. You are not what your clothes suggest that you are. Clothes never make the man. Some people dressed in rags are heavenly lights to those in darkness, and some dressed in the finest of clothing are rascals seeking to fleece the unfortunate. You are not what you eat. You are more than a mass of atoms. But you are your thoughts, because your thoughts are actually you. Just as it says in Book of Proverbs, "As a man thinketh in his heart, so is he!"

Man's greatest need is to think good thoughts. One night, the great astronomer Kepler spent an unusually long time on the roof of his house. On returning to his room, his wife asked him what he had been doing. He replied: "I have been thinking the thoughts of God." William Lyon Phelps said, "The happiest man is he who thinks the most interesting thoughts."

The quality in a person's thoughts determines the character of the person. There are negative thoughts of fear and worry that can haunt and depress a person to such an extent that he becomes miserable and useless. Attitudes and complexes are with us constantly. Good ones can be great companions to live with. Sir Sidney said, "They are never alone who are accompanied with noble thoughts." But, on the other hand, bad ones can cast us into dark shadows and deep valleys of despair. The base ignoble thoughts of a person reveal the size and stature of that person. Little people have small, self-centered thoughts. On the other hand, big people are mature and are concerned about others, and they are able to rise above the slime of evil thoughts.

Right thinking is the forerunner of good behavior. It is the prelude to words of wisdom and is more important than a reputation, because it is better to be a person of divine worth than to be respected by mortal man. Good thoughts are of greater value than good clothes, even the finest of woolen garments! It is more desirable than food, because man's life consists of more than physical bread!

What we do and think about today is perhaps the results of what we were thinking about yesterday, and what we will be doing tomorrow will be determined by our thoughts today. Where do you want your thoughts to take you?

Paul, of the New Testament, was a person who could live above circumstances. He could rejoice and be happy while tied to a ball and chain and guarded by a Roman soldier. Many had done Paul wrong, and he had suffered many injustices; but, he spent his time in prayer and thinking about the good things of life rather than trying to get even with the world, because he had learned the secret of lofty thinking.

The most important thing about you is your thoughts, because you, the real you, are your thoughts. So you may not be what you think you are, but what you think, you are. For "whatsoever a man thinketh in his heart, so is he."

The Moment Of Truth

I grew up on a farm in Jack County, located about midway between Wichita Fall and Fort Worth, Texas. Besides myself, there were my parents and my two older brothers. Our parents were godly people, and they gave us Christian teachings by word and action. I remember, however, that by the time I was a teenager, I thought that my mother was old-fashioned and outdated, and my dad taught us that work was for us all. On our small farm no one was unemployed!

Then, the day came for me to go to college. I was going to leave home and make my own decisions. The first few months were great—I was having a ball. I was doing great, but my lifestyle was changing. I had all the answers. I could now argue that it is not bad to drink a little. So I drank a couple of bottles of beer and actually tasted of whiskey. Then

about dancing— what was wrong with that? I wanted to be a popular guy, so I took ball room dancing as one of the P. E. courses. And really, is poker all that bad? We played with pennies, so it was not very expensive, which helped because I was working my way through college. So you see, with all my new activities, I was pretty busy and really did not have time to go to church.

Then it happened. The Good Lord zapped me. He gave me something to think about. A real struggle came to me about Jan. 27, 1940 to Feb. 2, 1940. I became obsessed with eternity! Students were going in all directions to class and other activities. And all I could think about was the idea of,

"Where are we going to spend eternity!" I had a miserable two or three weeks trying to make sense out of all these things. Then, when I surrendered to the will of the Lord, I received the peace that passes all understanding.

I went back to the farm for about a year and a half. I was restored to the fellowship of the Bethany Baptist Church Feb. 4, 1940, and I preached my first sermon March 3. My church licensed me to preach on April 14. The Lord had answered all my arguments for my desire to be worldly. I found out that there were many edifying things to do rather than dancing and playing poker. Those two bottles of beer and that sip of whiskey was just a trap of the Devil. After the Lord had restored me to sane thinking, I really found time to go to church, to pray, and to study the Scriptures. God can use the poor, the uneducated, and the weak. But God is holy, and those who serve him must be holy to be useful in his service. Then, I realized that Pa and Ma were not so dumb after all.

Thank You

We have many reasons to say "Thank You" and mean it. Our lives are a part of so many other lives that it would be very difficult for us to prosper or even survive without their help. Jeff D. Ray, a long time professor of Homiletics at Southwestern Baptist Theological Seminary, tells the story of a great artist giving an organ recital. It was in the day when someone was needed to pump in air behind the organ to make it operate. At the close of the first half of the recital, the audience gave an enthusiastic applause, and the organist said to his friend, "I seemed to have done a good job."

At the beginning of the second half of the recital, the organist pompously seated himself and pulled out the proper stops, adjusted the cuffs, and pressed down on the keys expecting a harmonious response. But not a sound came out. So he pulled out a few more stops and made some more adjustments and made another confident attack, but still no music. After a painful delay and a diligent investigation, the pumping helper was found laughing to himself. When the musician stormed at him he said, "You boasted awhile ago 'I did a good job.' I just wanted you to realize that you should have  used a plural pronoun. You can't get music out of the front end without some way to pump air into the back end."

Life is like that. We can do very little without the help of others. We are indebted to others, and without their help we would be doomed to failure. We are here today only by the grace of God. So we first must be thankful to the God who created us and sustains us each day. We should thank God for the health we have and the blessings of life that he gives us. I heard about a person who had toothaches so painfully that he thought everyone ought to be happy who did not have a toothache. Sometimes it takes sickness and pain to make us realize how precious good health can be. We need to say "Thank You," to so many people: to our parents who gave us tender care when we were too young to change our diapers, to our teachers who taught us, to the doctors who cared for us when we were sick, to the ministers who encouraged us, and to many more who have helped us along the way.

We just would not be able to survive by ourselves. We have so many people to thank. Like the musician who had to have the air pumper to make the music, we desperately need the help of others if we are going to be successful in whatever we do. So let us never forget the magic words, "Thank You."

Miss Edna

School days are times we never forget. My first year was at Winn Hill. The Winn Hill School was in the country in the County of Jack. Across the road was the Winn Hill Cemetery and Tabernacle, and across the creek was the Bethany Baptist Church. The schoolhouse had two rooms divided by a wall between them, but the north room was the only one being used at the time, and the school had only one teacher. In our room had long blackboard, and there was a big potbelly stove that burned wood for heat in the wintertime. In the entrance there was a cloakroom to hang our coats and a place to put our sack lunches.

The Winn Hill School taught the children beginning with the Primer and up through the seventh grade. Then, after finishing school at Winn Hill, the students went to Jermyn High School, which taught through the eleventh grade.

The one thing that impressed me most about the Winn Hill School was the teacher. Her name was Edna Meyers, but to us she was "Miss Edna." We had Arithmetic, English, and Reading, but I do not remember much else about the curriculum. However, I do remember that I had a hard time memorizing the Multiplication Table. For the Reading textbook, we had a classic — one of the best I have ever read. Its title was "Baby Ray." One of the things that I remember about Baby Ray was that he had a dog. He loved his dog so much that his dog loved him back! He had other animals also, and he loved all of them and they loved him. As I look back, I am reminded that Miss Edna had that same kind of love for us, and that is why we loved her so much. That was about 1926, and I have had many teachers over the years, but none was more important to me than my first teacher, Miss Edna.

Miss Edna was just out of college, and this was her first school to teach. What she lacked in experience, she provided in integrity, compassion, and intelligence, and a desire to bless the children she taught. She reminds me of a mother hen spreading her wings to cover her chicks.

At the close of the school day, often times a young man by the name of Fred Shields would be waiting to take her home. Later, he changed her name to "Shields," but she was and is to this day "Miss Edna" to me. Her children grew up and married, she became a grandmother, and her husband passed away, but she is still "Miss Edna" to me!

The one thing that I remember most about this special teacher was that she gave us little New Testaments. I had mine for many years, and I still carry it around in my mind and my heart. Is it not strange that now she would be in big trouble to give out Bibles that encourage the students to be holy, because now they are passing out condoms that encourage the students to be unholy! We have made a lot of improvements in the school system, but the outlawing of the Bible is not one of them. Praise God for teachers like "Miss Edna"!

Lost Without Knowing It

Have you ever been lost but did not know it? I was one time. I have thought about it many times, and I was really glad that I was found before I knew about it.

When I was a boy, we had revival meetings under tabernacles. The Methodists and Baptists would usually get together and invite a preacher to come for a week or two and preach under the tabernacle. It was an occasion for the whole community to come together for great revival meetings. A big revival meeting was in progress at Jermyn, Texas, which was four miles west of our farm. So our whole family—Pa, Ma, Anthony, Bus and I—went to the meeting one evening. The tabernacle was open on all sides, and the preacher would preach for a long time, so it was common for people to come in and go out during the time of preaching. My brothers, who were older than I, went outside, and I followed them. Our neighbor, Obert McCarty, was in his Model T Ford, which was parked a few feet from the tabernacle. While we were there with Obert, I crawled up in the back seat of his car and went to sleep. I do not remember anything else about the

preaching, but I went home with Obert in the back seat of his Model T Ford. He lived about five and a half miles east of Jermyn. I was lost but did not know it.

When church was over, I was nowhere to be found. People were sent out in every direction to look for me. Pa and Ma were upset, and no one could find me. In the meantime, Obert drove his car into his dark garage. Since he had put some mail in the back seat, he reached in the back seat to get his mail, and there he found me fast asleep. I have often thought about what I would have done if I had awakened in that dark garage sometime later in the night, several feet away from his house. That was quite a surprise for Obert, but when he found me there, he took me back to the tabernacle. Then my folks had a sign of relief, and the story had a happy ending.

There are many endings that are not so happy. Many people are lost but they do not know it. They are asleep but do not know it. Here is a person who has lost his way. He thinks that sensual pleasures are the purpose of life. He lives for pleasure and he thinks that the world owes him a living. In his promiscuous living, he has fathered children with no intention of being a father to them. Bad things have happened to him, because he has lost his way, but he still may not know about it. He wakes up in the middle of the night in that dark garage and wonders where he is. Life has gone sour. He has painted himself in a corner. In fact there are many in that same situation. We need to wake him and take him back to the tabernacle.

Limited Knowledge

There are so many things to know, and there is such a short time in which to learn them, that the unavoidable result for us all is limited knowledge, even in our own chosen field of endeavor. Whether it is in the field of medicine, or physical science, or sociology, we know so little, and the field is so great. Even in the knowledge of our personal relationships, even our next of kin, again we only have a limited knowledge.

What about the evaluation of the people we associate with each day? We all make daily evaluations of others. We perhaps start with the evaluation of physical appearance, such as neatness or posture. Then after we observe other traits such as the words used in speech and the attitude and disposition, we think we have the person "pegged."

I am reminded of Lucy in the Peanuts Cartoon when she says, "I have a knack of finding faults in others." Then when big brother asks her about what she does about her own faults, she says, "I have a knack of overlooking them." It is strange that we know so little about our neighbor, and yet we often think that he needs to make so many changes. On the other hand, we know so much about ourselves, but we are not so interested in making any changes in our own behavior.

I was taught a great lesson in evaluating the behavior of others in the year 1944. I was pastor of the First Baptist Church at Sullivan City, and Jack Brady was one of our deacons. We had a windmill by the church that needed to be repaired. So Jack and I climbed upon the tower under the big wheel to make the repair. And it was under that big wheel that I received the lesson that is still with me. Jack started to tell me about his neighbor, but before he finished his first sentence he stopped himself and said, "I don't know enough about that man to talk about him." Then he changed the subject and never said another word about his neighbor. That has been more than a half a century ago, and I have no idea about what Jack was going to say about his neighbor, but those words have echoed a thousand times since in my ears: "I don't know enough about that man to talk about him." Thank you Jack for the lesson you taught me that day on the windmill tower under the big wheel!

Help

Have you ever needed help badly? We are social beings, and we cannot survive very long without some help from others. Just a few days ago I had to call 911 for my wife, who was in a dangerous physical condition. In my own case, I have had the need of help, such as in the case of overspending and needing financial help; and, I know what it means to be stuck in a mud hole in an automobile!

The world is filled with people who need help. Perhaps the reason why the Bible story of the Good Samaritan thrills us so much is because the hero of the story went out of his way to help the dying man who had been robbed. The priest and the Levite passed by on the other side, but the Samaritan—to the Jew, the wrong nationality, the wrong color, and the wrong race—was the hero. His compassion for the one in need, regardless, caused him to go to the other side of the road and give aid to the dying man on that road to Jericho.

It was the year 1959 when I was in desperate need for someone to help me. I left my family at Harlingen, Texas, and I was assigned to Misawa Air Base, Japan. Our cars arrived at  Hachinohe, Japan, and we were sent by military bus to get them. After a long ride on a bumpy bus and a winding and dusty road, we finally went through the city and over a bridge to where our cars were located. The bus left and we all got into our cars. Then, all the others with their cars drove up the hill and out of sight. My car started, but then it stalled out and would not go. There I was! The sun was a little above the western horizon. And dropping fast! We had been in a bloody war with Japan, and I had just arrived in Japan. Now there was no one but Japanese people around me. I did not know how to speak Japanese, so there was no way that I could communicate. Everyone had left me, and I had no idea of how to get back to the base. I was half a world away from home. I was devastated! Just before the sun tipped over the horizon, I heard a helicopter, and it landed near me. An Air Force pilot got out of the helicopter and went to his car that was nearby. He had come to pick up his car. He was the "Good Samaritan" who came to rescue me. What a relief! It still thrills me to see him coming toward me, and I have relived that experience many times. I do not remember his name, but I will never forget his kindness and help. I remember that he was about my size, he was a pilot, he was kind and benevolent, and he was black.

Let us be mindful of people who need help. If we turn aside to help someone in need, that might be more important than what we had planned for the day. The Good Samaritan was on a business trip somewhere beyond Jericho, and, praise the Lord, he had time to help someone in great need. May we go and do likewise.

Grandpa's Advice

When I was a boy, I used to go visit with Grandpa and Grandma Wilton, who lived about a half mile west of our house. In the wintertime, we would hover around the wood stove in the living room to keep warm. They always had good advice, and I remember that on one occasion, Grandpa told me about a life changing experience that he had.

Grandpa (whose real name was Henry Franklin Wilton and who was known to most people as "Uncle Henry") had some interesting stories to share with us. One of those stores become a part my memory never to be erased. It all happened at harvest time.

There was a revival meeting in the community with an evangelist on the message of the gospel of eternal life. Grandpa and his neighbor met to talk awhile at the fence line of the farms. The neighbor told Grandpa about the wonderful protracted meeting, and he invited Grandpa to come and join them for a great spiritual blessing. Grandpa told him that it was harvest time and that the cotton needed to be picked, so he just did not have time to go to the meeting. Then the neighbor told him that he thought that if he could get to heaven, along with all his family, that would be more important than all the cotton in the community. After Grandpa thought about what he had been told, he came to the conclusion that his neighbor was right. So he accepted the advice of his friend and went to the meeting; and, some of the members of Grandpa's household had life changing experiences during that revival. He was always grateful for the advice that he received that day.

That day, as we hovered around the wood burning stove in his living room, I also took the advice of that good man who had given Grandpa that advice many years before. I was richer and wiser when I returned home that day. I still gather around that stove as I did when I was a young boy on that winter day and listen again to that beautiful story. There is lots of advice from people all around us. Let us be careful to reject the bad and accept the good!

Grandpa's Experience

Grandpa Wilton had some interesting experiences to tell us. He was not a man with a lot of schooling, but he was a person of intelligence and wisdom. His words were not big, but he had many interesting things to tell us. He never used vulgarity or curse words, but he always had words of encouragement. His friends called him "Uncle Henry."

One of his favorite stories was about the time he first saw an automobile. Grandpa lived way out in "the sticks." His house was about 4 miles east of Jermyn, Texas and about 12 miles west of Jacksboro, Texas, the county seat of Jack County. The road that passed by his house was a dirt road that snaked its way from Jermyn to Jacksboro.

Grandpa took a weekly newspaper, The Cappers Weekly, that gave him some information about current events. So he had read about a new vehicle that would run without a horse or mule. He had a wagon to work in the fields, and he had a nice buggy for transportation, but this idea about a horseless carriage was quite fascinating to him. He was interested in seeing one someday.

And one day it happened on that road in front of his house! A man drove up in one of those horseless carriages, and steam was going up out of the radiator like a steam engine. The man stopped at the yard gate in front of his house just a few feet from the porch. The man was in need of water for his car, and he asked Grandpa if he could help him. Grandpa was an accommodating man, so he was quick to tell him that he would be glad to get him some water.

North Creek wandered through his farm, and it usually had waterholes in it. Grandpa knew of a place in the creek that had lots of water that was only about a quarter of a mile from his house. So he got a bucket and told him he would go with him to get the water. So Grandpa actually got to ride in this horseless carriage. They went to the waterhole and got the water, and the man used a bucketful to fill up his radiator. He thanked Grandpa for the water, but Grandpa was puzzled, because it took only a bucketful to fill it. With astonishment, he said, "That won't make enough steam for anything!"

To this, the man replied to him, "This car does not run on steam. It runs on gasoline."

Grandpa answered, "Well, Pshaw! If I had known that, we could have gotten that much water from my well!"

Christmas 2001

Christmas is coming once more. The year 2000 came, and the sun is still coming up in the East and going down in the West, and the world did not end as some who claimed to know were prophesying. This should make us realize that we need to work on His time schedule, as regards His coming here or our going there. As we prepare for the Christmas Celebration, let us remember Jesus, the real reason for the season, whose humble birth was on that first Christmas Day.

Christmas was the biggest day of the year for us who lived out in the "sticks" near a little town called Jermyn, Texas. We prepared for the occasion by getting gifts for our friends and wondering what gifts we might receive from our friends. Our parents would prepare by getting extra food for the season. This one time of the year we usually had apples, oranges, walnuts, almonds, and coconuts. Of course, Santa Claus would deliver all the gifts on   Christmas Eve about midnight. And Santa Claus always came on the eve of the birthday of Jesus. In Sunday School we were told about the birth of Jesus, but our attention was on Santa Claus. He was a real friend to me. My dream world was shattered when I heard my cousins talking about Santa Claus and saying that he was no real person and that our gifts were provided by our parents. How could that be? Didn't I see the tracks of the reindeers in our front yard early one Christmas morning! I did not want to believe what they said. But facts often shatter our dreams.

So the important thing about December 25 was that it was the birthday of Jesus. So that was something to emphasize and celebrate the day by honoring Jesus and giving gifts to one another. Then some smart guy came up with the idea that the 25th of December was not the birthday of Jesus, because he was not even born in December. And we were also told that there was a time when the many members of the church were slaves and they could not have a special day to worship. But the 25th of December was a pagan holiday, and everyone was given that day off to celebrate. So I am told that the church came up with that day to observe the birth of Jesus, so the slaves would have an opportunity to be a part of the great celebration. That used to bother me, but really it doesn't bother me anymore. I am convinced that Jesus was not born in December, but that fact is also not important anymore. But the fact that Jesus came and gave his life a ransom for us does make the difference. So I am not certain about the exact day of the birth of Jesus, but I am certain that 25 December was the birthday of Grandpa Henry Franklin Wilton. And we used to meet on Christmas Day to celebrate his birthday and the birthday of Jesus.

So here it is Christmas time again, and we are thrilled with the idea of Jesus being born in Bethlehem, with the story of the Shepherds and the Wise Men coming to fall at his feet. The gift of salvation that he offers is so much more than we could ever imagine that Santa Claus could give. And about the exact date. What difference does that make? Praise the Lord he came and we are told that he is coming again! Let's be ready to meet him when he comes!

Blessings on you for a great Christmas season.

Changing the Price Tags

The Danish philosopher Soren Kierkegaard tells a parable of a man who broke into a department store one night. Rather than stealing merchandise, he rearranged the price tags on many items. The next morning the clerks and customers found one surprise after another: diamond necklaces for a dollar and cheap costume jewelry costing thousands of dollars.

That seems to be what has happened to our country. The price tags have been rearranged so that what used to be cheap has been given an expensive price tag, and that which used to be precious is no longer regarded as of great value. Even the members of the church have helped to rearrange the price tags. Statistics indicate that the standards and the behavior of the members of the church are about the same as the standards and the behavior of the world. Such moral issues as abortion, sexual perversion, murder, drugs, alcohol, and thievery should be clear and steadfast in the thinking of the child of God. But the statistics indicate that there is no difference!

The people underestimated faith and the laws of God. They have devalued virtue and inflated evil. We are reminded of the people in days of Isaiah: "Ah, you who call evil good and good evil, who put darkness for light and light for darkness, who put bitter for sweet and sweet for bitter!" (Isa 5:20). And they overpriced their own wisdom and cleverness: "Ah, you who are wise in your own eyes, and shrewd in your own sight!" (Isa 5:21).

Have we become more concerned with wealth than righteousness? We have tried to junk the Bible and replace it with the philosophies of worldly men. Our heroes have been sports figures regardless of their moral values. Again we are reminded of the people in Isaiah's day. He said that they made heroes of heavy drinkers. "Ah, you who are heroes in drinking wine and valiant at mixing drink" (Isa 5:22). And bribery subverted justice. "Ah, you who acquit the guilty for a bribe, and deprive the innocent of their rights!" (Isa 5:23).

God has blessed our land in so many ways. We have the wealth of the nations; yet we often sell our heritage for worthless junk. God has created a climate for goodness, but we, as well as the people in Isaiah's day, have cultivated weeds and produced moral confusion: "He dug it and cleared it of stones, and planted it with choice vines; he built a watchtower in the midst of it, and hewed out a wine vat in it; he expected it to yield grapes, but it yielded wild grapes." (Isa 5:2).

Yes, our price tags have been changed! Goodness has been exchanged with smartness, justice with bribery, sobriety with excitement, wisdom with education, virtue with experience, honesty with success, integrity with hypocrisy, and the mind of God with the mind of man.

The Fast Time Period

We are living in a fast time period—fast food, fast cars, fast communications, etc. We do not like to wait for everything. We want it to happen now! In fact we are going so fast that we often forget to smell the roses as we pass by. But I grew up before the acceleration of so much speed.

Yes, I grew up "in the sticks." My little world consisted of Pa and Ma and two brothers. Grandpa and Grandma lived about a half-mile to the west; over the hill about a mile northwest was where the Kinnards and the Hubers lived; to the east about ¾ of a mile over the Easter Hill was where Ernest Easter and his mother lived. And back to the south there was nothing but trees and bushes and rocks. It was just a wooded area that went on and on. We lived so far out in the country that we did not need to be in a hurry. The cows were there to give us milk, the hogs were there to give  us meat, and the garden was just about 10 or 15 feet from the hen house. Our workplace was just on the other side of the cow lot, so we did not need transportation to take us to work. My Dad thought the workday was from sunup until sundown. There was plenty to do, so why get in a hurry?

We went to the "Big City" about twice each month to get a supply of groceries, such things as flour, cornmeal, sugar, salt, pepper, soap, and black draught for the medicine drawer. Jacksboro—about 12 miles east of our farm—was the county seat of Jack County, and it was a pretty large city, because it had about half of all 8000 people in Jack County. They even put in a movie house on the second floor of the Spears Drug Store. For 10 or 15 cents, a person could see the Saturday afternoon matinee. And Saturday afternoon was a time that I looked forward to, because Herbert, my cousin, would probably be there also. We could go up and down the streets of Jacksboro, and if we had five cents we could get a hamburger. Yes! Those were days to remember!

We did not have a communication problem, because we could write a letter and send it anywhere in the United States for 2 cents, and a post card was only a penny. We had a telephone line hooked up to Grandma's house, which was about a half mile away, and I can remember that at one time we were hooked up all the way to Uncle Jake's house, which was about 3 miles to the West. It was hard to keep that line up, so we were not connected with Uncle Jake and Aunt Amy very much of the time. Our telephone was a big rectangular red box about 2 feet high and about 1 foot wide. We had to put two large B batteries about the size of a  pickle jar in the telephone box to keep it working. With the small crank that was located on the side of the box, we could ring up and get Grandma most anytime. It was quite a fascinating invention. And we were excited about having it!

That was the world that I grew up in, so I am not too excited about this fast living. Rather than going to some fast food place, I am content to just put some beans in the crock pot in the morning, let them cook all day, and then just enjoy a great bean banquet in the evening! To me, it just "doesn't get any better than that!"

Ancient Code Provides
Rules For Today's Life

There is a story of a certain master and slave who years ago went deep-sea fishing. When they were making their way back to shore late in the night, the master became sleepy and turned the helm over to his faithful servant, Mose. Before doing this, however, he pointed out the North Star to Mose and urged him to keep his eye on it. But the master had not been asleep very long before Mose also went to sleep. When he awakened he was in utter confusion. He called to his master frantically. "Wake up!" he said, and show me another star, I've done run clean past that one!" Many feel this way about the "Ten Commandments" of the Old Testament, but, it is my conviction that we can no more run past this ancient code than we can run past the North Star.

The Ten Commandments were written on two tablets of stone. One tablet had those commandments that have to do with our relationship to our God; the other tablet had those commandments that have to do with our relationship to our fellow man. Jesus summarized the "Commandments of God" in this way, "The Lord our God is one Lord...and thou shalt love the Lord thy God with all thy heart, and with all thy soul, and with all thy mind, and with all thy strength; ...and Thou shalt love thy neighbour as thyself."

Concerning the "Personal" Commandments, they are written in the second person singular. These Commandments are universal in scope, because they appeal to all individuals alike, regardless of social prestige or intellectual standing. They are prohibitive in form but affirmative in spirit. They regulate the internal. By taking out the bad, we have room for the good. In order to worship the One Truth God, we must forsake all false gods.

Rituals have come and gone, but moral law abides forever. It shall always be the right thing to serve God and man. We shall never be able to abolish or disregard them because they are as fundamental to basic morality as the multiplication table is to arithmetic. If you would like to read them you can find them in your Bible in the 20th chapter of Exodus.

Conquer Tensions by
Divine Rejuvenation

Have you ever felt tense and "all tied up in a knot?" If you have not, you are certainly an abnormal person, because there are times when most people feel that way. People act differently when under stress; some are like a "bull in a China closet"; others are a little more cautious about giving vent to their emotional feelings.

Some of the emotions that are common to most individuals are anger, hatred, lust, arrogance, and covetousness. These attitudes usually appear ugly when detected in the other person, but often they are allowed to remain and grow in the atmosphere of our own mental thoughts.

When the build-up comes from the inside, there may be an outward expression, if there is no way to drain off the tension. It is like steam in a teakettle; it needs a stopgap, or it might blow the lid off the kettle.

It is interesting to ponder the question, "why the tension?" We are a bundle of complexes and goals, each one having his individual peculiarities, but wanting to achieve status in his own eyes and in the eyes of others. He may think that to gain status he must have money, rank, degrees in education, or social prestige. He may have complexes that tell him that the world is against him; so, with a "chip on the shoulder" he goes out to fight anyone who stands in his way. His early conditioning can be a help to him, or it may be a hindrance all through life. His goal can become his god, and anything that stands in his way of achieving it becomes his enemy. This objective is only temporary and never brings real security; there is constant fear and anxiety connected with it. Just a few can reach the height of worldly goals, and when they do, they discover them to be only illusions and disappointments.

There are some very practical ways in which to drain out these tensions of life. It is necessary to have goals of eternal value. The emphasis in everyone's life ought to be one's personal integrity rather than the attainment of goals or  certain appendixes to life. Life itself becomes the focal point. The Divine Breath of God becomes more important than the "gaining of the world" or the ruling of the universe. When a person has learned the art of living in peace with himself, then he can live in harmony with his neighbor. His goals can be achieved, because by the grace of God, everyone can fill his life with eternal values — it is a free gift to all. When, through the power of Divine rejuvenation, we have exchanged anger for understanding, hatred for love, lust for purity, arrogance for humility, covetousness for thankfulness, and faith for anxiety, then our tensions will disappear and we can live at peace with ourselves as well as with our neighbor.

Sacrifices And Conveniences

Sacrifice is the big word in every religion, but people everywhere are trying to find a religion of convenience.

In the matter of giving to the Lord's Work—I want to give, but after I have taken out for my necessities and luxuries. If there is any left over, the Lord can have it, because I think it is a grand thing to give.

In the matter of church attendance—I think everyone ought to go to church, because that is the socially acceptable thing to do. I will go regularly—if it is convenient. Worship service should not be too early—because Sunday is the only day I can "sack in" late. It ought not to be too late—because I "must" eat dinner at "straight up" twelve on Sunday. It is always so nice to get out to the golf course early, or the picnic grounds, or somewhere else. Maybe, about the middle of the afternoon would be a good time—but on second thought that would not be a good time, because I would be out "enjoying myself" at that time.

Sunday night is no good for a church service, because the "kids" have to get up early for school Monday morning, so I must get to bed early—that is, if I don't decide to go to a movie or go visit the Jones' or go for a late evening drive. Come to think of it, there is no real convenient time every Sunday, so I will go just when I can "sandwich" it in between more "important" activities.

We are told in Biblical history that one man was looking for a "convenient season" to accept his religious responsibility. There is no indication that he ever found it. The Bible pictures the "Kingdom of God" as a pearl of great price which could not be obtained unless the purchaser was willing to give all his lesser pearls. So it is today.

If a person is not willing to make a sacrifice—to give all—then the Kingdom of God cannot be a reality in his or her life. The big, startling fact about sacrificing for God is that it is impossible to make a real sacrifice, because when a person tries, his reward is so great that the sacrifice seems as nothing. You who have made that personal commitment know what I am talking about. You know the futility of seeking a religion of convenience, because that kind of religion is never more that a superficial attempt to "hoodwink" self or society.

'Best Seller' Authored
By 44 Over 2000 Years

Reading is one of the great blessings to be enjoyed by men. The bookstores are filled with all kinds of reading material. Some are good, and some are trash; some lift the thoughts of readers to lofty heights; others contaminate the imagination with filthy intentions.

The book that I would like to recommend to you for your sincere consideration was a best seller last year. In fact,  it has been a best seller now for quite some time. This book is an unusual one. About 2,000 years of preparation were required to get it ready for the press. It has about 44 authors, and yet there is a central theme all through the book.

It is a book of such importance that William Lyons Phelps of Yale University once said: "I believe knowledge of the Bible without a college course is more valuable than a college course without the Bible." Yes, the book I refer to is the Bible.

The Bible is a library within itself. It is divided into two big parts: the Old Testament and the New Testament. In the Old Testament, we are told about the world's beginning and the creation of mankind. There are several books of ancient history in which God's chosen people had a great part to play. It is filled with romance, thrills, and adventure.

The New Testament tells about the birth and life of Jesus. It tells how he established His church and commissioned His disciples to go into the entire world and preach the gospel of good news, and It tells about the disciples giving their lives for a cause that they considered greater than themselves. The Bible has changed the lives of millions. It has a message for every person who has ever lived. Therefore, it has a message for you!

Say, do you have a copy of this book? They are published in most every dialect and language in the world. There are many translations of the English Bible. They cost from 25 cents to 40 or 50 dollars, depending upon the quality of the binding.

Oh yes, that reminds me, I have an extra one that I will give you if you will stop by and pick it up. I hope you enjoy reading this 2002 Best Seller!

Christianity Provides
Moral Law Foundation

There have been many philosophies of life since the beginning of time; there are many today. Some of the old ones have only changed names but are basically the same. In a broad sense, we might say there are only two: the philosophy that centers on the idea of selfishness, and the philosophy of life that centers on moral principles.

The world can be divided into the two ideologies today: Communism and Christianity. It would not be fair to say that everything in Communism is bad, but it is an ideology that is basically wrong because it leaves out the elemental principles of morality. The foundation for the societies of the Western World is basically religious. However, this does not mean that our ideology is without flaws, but it does mean that we have some eternal principles on which to build a better society. In the last decade, many governments have fallen; colonialism is on its way out in many places in the world; nationalism is popular the world over. People everywhere want political freedom.

In many places in the world, political bondage and social prestige based on prejudice, along with other injustices, have been associated with some form of religion. Therefore, some nations in their attempt to gain freedom have looked to the strong power of Communism to deliver them. In their struggle against the evils of their society, they have fallen an easy prey to the Soviet Giant. A very wise man many years ago said, "Righteousness exalteth a nation, but sin is a reproach to any people." This is an eternal principle. A nation built on moral principles need never fear, but the disregard of the moral law, which is one meaning of sin, causes deterioration and collapse.

This world of ours needs reconstructing, but unless it has a foundation based on moral law, all efforts are in vain.

Each of us, in our own little niche, can make the world a better place in which to live. This is not done by closing our eyes to the evils of our own society, but it is done by working in our own society to eliminate the bad and amplify the good. Therefore, may we rejoice with the peoples of the world who want a better world, and may we lend our hand in bringing it about. May we also remember that in a society where peace and tranquility reign, there must be truth and righteousness, and these are moral concepts. If we start here, and build thereon, we can indeed have a better world in which to live.

Abundant Living
Through Spiritual Maturity

Everyone has the ability to become a better person. Man is born in the image of God; therefore, he has the potential for a personality of goodness. However, man is free to make his choice—which also suggests the possibility of choosing the bad instead of the good. Thus it becomes the perennial task of everyone to strive to suppress the bad and cultivate the good that is within.

We admire great personalities and would like to be like them. People of great personalities did not drift into maturity, but they grew to greatness through intelligent and persistent effort.

One of the first things to do in preparation for emotional growth is to take an objective view of self. It is easy to see the virtue or evil in others, but it is hard to make a true evaluation of our own lives. It becomes the pastime of too many to verbally evaluate the conduct of others; it is much less common for a person to examine his own behavior.

Much can be done about a person's spiritual maturity. The Bible is a good book to help to make a wise appraisal of our lives, because it is easy to see ourselves in this divine book. It is the textbook for goodness and morality. What the multiplication table is to arithmetic and the alphabet is to reading, the Bible is to the school of abundant living.

When we see what we could be—by the grace of God, and then see what we are, we are reminded of the great progress that should be made. Achievement in Christian growth, as well as achievement in any other area of endeavor, can be made through consistent effort. When we become serious in this worthy task, we will see the stupidity of forever judging the actions of others. Only after our own lives become noble and enriched will we be able to help others, and that by example rather than by criticism. May this be the task for all of us who are less than perfect!

Art Of Helping Others
Brings Vast Dividends

A blind man came to a washed-out bridge in his long and tiresome journey. The detoured trail was rough and dangerous, and he did not know how to cross the treacherous stream. At this junction of the road there was also a lame man who was hardly able to drag himself along. He, too, was unable to cross the stream. The blind man asked the lame man for help. After careful consideration, they decided to cross the stream together. The blind man was strong, so he was feet to the lame man; the lame man had good eyes, so he was eyes to the blind man. With this mutual helpfulness, they traveled on their way with safety and pleasure.

We live in a world that has much sorrow and need. Thousands of people starve to death each year; some are despondent and defeated; many are diseased and degraded; while, a few are successful and happy. Some are young; some are in the prime of life; and, others are old. However, regardless of the circumstances, you may be sure that everyone you meet has some kind of a problem to work out in his or her daily living.

In this modern world we live in, we are dependent on others to supplement our daily activities. We do not have the material resources for our survival, so we must go to the grocery store to fill our cupboards. We are dependent on our cars for transportation, and we must go to the filling station to get gasoline to operate our cars. We are dependent on the telephone and our cell phones, so we must pay for these services. In the entertainment world, we must pay to keep our cable TV and Internet connected to the world. We must call on clothing stores to supply us with clothes to wear. We need Doctors to advise us and give us medicine. In our spiritual needs, the church can be the support we need in prayer, compassion, and fellowship.

We must depend on others for our daily needs, and just as the lame man and the blind man could not cross the stream without one another's help, so are we dependent upon one another. Let us be alert to the needs of others. With spiritual help, we can be partners in this venture of life, and while we bless them, we will be blessed by others.

Happiness: The Key Could
Be In the Present, Not The Future

The search for happiness is a universal search— everyone wants to live in a state of happiness, and no one wants to live in a state of confusion and unhappiness. People everywhere are hoping and working for this time to come in their lives. However, to the majority of the world's people, this never comes! Could it be that the search is pursued in the wrong direction?

In relation to time, some try to live in the past, and others try to live in the future, while both miss the opportunity of enjoying the present. The little boy projects into the future and imagines his goal will be reached when he grows up into manhood like his Dad. Dad, in his memory of days gone by, looks at the "ole swimming hole" or the first time he held Mom's hand as the "good old days." There have been many critical times in the history of the world, but there have been individuals in every generation who enjoyed living.

Some people think that the place a person lives is the deciding factor in happiness. The countryman looks to the  city, desiring a life of activity, and the city man looks to the country, desiring a life of privacy. The tired businessman thinks that life would be perfect if he could only have a vacation in Hawaii; and, the average military person, especially if stationed overseas, knows that everything would be just right if he could only get back home to see his friends and family. The fact remains that some people are happy in every part of the world, while others in the same locality are not.

The writer of sacred writ once said, "Happy is the man that findeth wisdom." Wisdom, in the Bible, is related to God. So, does this not mean that happiness is a by-product, and we find it by finding God and His will for us? Therefore, the age in which we live, or the locality of our residence is of very little importance as compared to our mental attitude.

Happiness is within your reach. May you find this road and travel it with persistence.

A Quality Thought Process,
A Key to Quality Life
Clyde C. Wilton

Thinking is hard work, and sometimes dangerous; therefore, few people indulge in it. People are born into a certain culture, and they are apt to accept the status quo without hesitation. This is the lot of the masses. However, each generation produces a few individuals who think for themselves. These are the people who change society.

In the city of Athens, Greece, there was a man near the end of the Fifth Century B.C. whose influence changed the whole course of human thought. He received the ordinary  training of a Greek boy and was taught the trade of his father. He was awkward, with a squat figure, short neck, bald head, a thick upturned nose, and round prominent eyes. He wore a single rough woolen garment and never wore shoes. Who was this unusual man who thought for himself? You are right—his name was Socrates.

Socrates refused to let others do his thinking. He was a good citizen, and he served his country well, but he never allowed conventional standards to deflect him from his clear concept of just conduct. This "heresy" was considered to be a dangerous corrupting influence on the youth of the city. Thus, Socrates was sentenced to die by drinking hemlock poison. The political leaders were able to put him to death, but they were unable to kill his influence.

Individual thought is a God-given privilege and responsibility. True, it is hard work and sometimes very dangerous, especially if you "think out loud." Many thinkers, in the realm of politics as well as religion, have forfeited their lives for this privilege. The greatest blessing of life is to live in the realm of lofty thoughts. It is a luxury we need not do without. All progress has been made in science and religion by people who use this God-given ability to think clear and wholesome thoughts. It makes the difference between success and defeat, joy and sorrow, progress and stagnation.

Are you willing to do a little individual thinking? If so, who knows, you may come up with an idea that will change the course of the modern world! The world is always in need of straight thinkers like Socrates. Luck to you—and may you not "lose your neck" in this worthy adventure!

Easter Points to Time
For Spiritual Growth

Easter season is here again. May this be a time for us to think in terms of spiritual growth? The word "Easter" is not in the original writings of Holy Scripture. It comes from the word "eastre," which was the name of an ancient Teutonic goddess of spring. This day has been set aside by the Christian churches as a very holy day, because it commemorates the resurrection of Our Lord Jesus the Christ. It is quite obvious that the role of Bunny Cottontail, with his colorful eggs and the much-emphasized Eater Parade, has sometimes "stolen the show." Easter is a religious day, and may we ever remember this most important fact. Jesus arose from the dead some two thousand years ago and demonstrated to the world the fact that man is an immortal soul.

There are many interesting things about the Eastern World. Among some of the most spectacular things of the East are the tombs of the past monarchs. I shall never forget

visiting the Taj Mahal. This mausoleum was built for Mumtaz Mahal, the wife of Shah Jahan. What a construction job this was! Nearly 20,000 men were employed in the building of this tomb. It was begun in 1531 and completed 22 years later. This is a memorial which has had no equal in the history of any nation. It is one of the seven wonders of the modern world.

It was my privilege on another day to stand on the top of one of the highest pyramids in Egypt — another tomb with a message of the past. It was a construction of stupendous magnitude that took thousands of slaves several years to construct! This was the tomb for the body of an ancient Pharaoh of Egypt. No doubt Moses saw this pyramid when he was a bond-servant in Egypt.

There is another tomb in the East that has more meaning than all the other tombs in the world; it is the empty tomb in the old city of Jerusalem. I can still see it! It was a tomb hewn out of rock that had belonged to Joseph of Arimathea, who was willing for Jesus to us it. Jesus, the ever-living King of all Kings, does not need a mausoleum to acclaim His greatness. This empty tomb does not speak of the past like the Taj Mahal and the Pyramids of Egypt, but it speaks of the future. Jesus arose from the dead on that first Easter Morning, and He assured us of victory over the grave if we trust in Him and His way of Life. This is what Easter should mean to each of us!

Marital Problems

Where would you go, if you should some day have a marital problem? You might go to your neighbor, but very likely he or she could not be of much help—except to sympathize. You might go to your mother, and she would agree with you, but that might intensify the problem. You might go to your spouse, but very likely he or she is emotionally involved in the conflict. You might go to your minister, and he could tell you the moral implications involved, but that might not be what you need to solve the problem. You might go to your lawyer, and he could tell you what your legal rights are, but that would be of little help if you were interested in salvaging your marriage.

You might go to your doctor, and he could tell you about the physical body, but that would also be of little help, because 95% of marital discord is psychological rather than physical—even in the cases of frigidity. You might go to a marriage counselor, if you could find one, and if you had the time and money. The marriage counselor very likely could help you—but not with a magic word! He or she will not attempt to—if so, consider that counselor a fake and seek another! The wise counselor will attempt to help you find the solution to your problem, by certain laws of cause and effect.

Why do people "fall in love" with one another? What gives them that feeling of romance so much that they must be in the presence of the other! The answer is simple enough, the law of cause and effect. Why is love so blind? They get married and live happily ever after—hardly so! It is not as easy as the storybook or the screen pictures it. After a while of marital ecstasy, life becomes real again, and they find that they are living with a person instead of an ideal—a person less than the ideal, sometimes much less! Why does this happen? Simple enough—the law of cause and effect!

The ideal marriage is a lifetime commitment. How long will the marriage partners be "in love"? I think that I have found the answer. They will be "in love" so long as they meet one another's psychological needs. If the marriage  partners are more interested in meeting the other's needs rather than their own selfish, self-centered desires, the marriage will be more stable. In that case the avenues of communication will be opened up. And if the marriage partners can really communicate with one another, their problems can be worked out. In that case there will be no need for a third-party counselor.

Marriage is a wonderful relationship to those who are mature enough to accept the responsibilities, as well as the privileges, of marriage. If marriage is what it is supposed to be, the end is even sweeter than the beginning. Blessings on you for a wonderful marriage!

Military Service Seen
As Test Of Character

The military service is often the crucial time for the testing of character. We were reared in a society of restrictions. When people enter military service, they leave  home and many of their constraining influences behind. The new life that they enter into becomes a time of testing of their moral fiber. If character is going to be maintained, it must be made of "sterner stuff" than outward restrictions. Their lives must be founded on positive convictions rather than negative prohibitions. It is then that the parents back home can see whether they have adequately prepared their son or daughter to meet life in all its complexities.

The military service is often blamed for the moral breakdown of many of our young men and women, but more often it should be placed on the home, because there is where the early formative period of life is spent. It is so easy to "pass the buck," even in this ideal of moral responsibility. It is true that when many go out on their own at this age, they go the way of evil rather than good. However, this is not just indicative of military life, but it is true in other communities where work is of a transitory nature.

The way of good goes through every community, as well as evil; however, it is not as broad and colorful to most people, perhaps, but always there, nevertheless. The attitude before World War II was that military life will be degrading to the personnel, but we will try not to ruin them; the philosophy developed during World War II was that we ought to send them back to civilian life as good as they were before entering the service; and, the objective now is to give them opportunities for growth to maturity and to send them back to civilian life as better individuals than they were when they entered the service. The military offers many opportunities for character development, such as: a program of education, a program of recreation, a program of moral and religious instructions, a program of various social and cultural activities, and a program of upgrading in each person's particular work. Yes, there are many everyday opportunities for character development, if we only look  for them. It might be easier to say that military life is "lousy" and degrading, but it is wiser to accept the many opportunities we have for a fuller and more satisfying life.

There is a long period of training before the prize fighter goes into the ring to fight; there ought to be a period of "training unto godliness" from the cradle to the period of military life. With a good foundation in Christian morals, the young adult can learn to be a person of integrity—regardless of the attending circumstances. Even without this foundation, the case is not hopeless if the individual will accept certain moral and spiritual precepts that filter out the bad and retain the good in everyday experiences. Regardless of the peak you stand on, the sensible thing is to take the path of Eternal Light rather than the broad way that leads to darkness.

Peace For Individual, World
Starts With Self

Peace is a word that is used often. It expresses the desire of the peoples of the world. We all wish for a time when all nations would "beat their swords into plowshares." This would indicate a mutual love, trust, and respect between the nations, creeds, and nationalities. This is a goal that each of us ought to personally interested in.

The world is big, with millions of peoples, and our voice is usually lost in the cry of the masses. We do, however, have a realm of influence, and we ought to be interested in doing something of permanent good in this realm.

The most significant achievement for each of is within our own soul or self. Unless we conquer in this citadel, we will likely fail in all others. To conquer here is to have the peace of mind that goes beyond human understanding. It is the peace that permits a person to enjoy living with himself. He may then realize that he has stood for what he believes to be truth and goodness. He has accepted in his life an abstract God, which has given him the ability to accept himself. He has surrendered all ill will, hatred, and greed to his Maker and has received in return good will, love, and kindness, which gives peace to the human soul.

Do you have this peace? It can be yours! If all the individuals of the world had this peace, the world could live without war and strife. So, may we start and make over the world, and begin with ourselves!

Personal Security Is Based
On Trust In God

What is your personal security? Are you prepared to meet life with all its blessings and all its sorrows? What do you put your trust in? The Psalmist puts his trust in God. He says: "The Lord is my Shepherd; I shall not want." David, the king of Israel, was supposedly the author of this psalm. He had great wealth, but he did not say that great wealth was his security. He had political power, but he did not say political power was his security. David knew that all temporal things were transient and were soon to pass away, so if he was going to have real lasting security he must put his faith in the Eternal. So it is that all thinking people must realize that Eternal Security is to be found only in the Eternal God.

If you can say the first part of that Bible verse, "The Lord is my Shepherd," then you can say the remainder of the verse, "I shall not want." David continues to explain in the rest of the chapter this idea of security. "He leadeth me beside the water of rest" is indicative of the peace of mind that one finds in God. Many people seek it elsewhere, but alas! Their search is in vain!

The Lord leads only "in paths of righteousness." So watch your step, my friend! The Lord wants you to have the best in life, and He is ever pointing us in that direction. The spiritual "green pastures" of this psalm are vastly more important than the cattle upon a thousand hills and the world's supply of the silver and the gold.

There will be days of gloom, when you "walk through the valley of the shadow of death," but it will not be bad if the Lord is the Shepherd of your soul. This sweet morsel of truth has been a wonderful comfort to millions of peoples of the world. Just in case you would like to read the entire Psalm, it is the Twenty-Third.

Early Start In Setting
Spiritual Example Cited

We are born imitators. We learned to do by concrete example before we were taught by abstract ideas. Therefore, it is very important that we provide the right example for our children. Warden Lawes of Sing Sing Penitentiary said: "When we get to the place where we pay more attention to the high chair, we will have less need for the electric chair."

A woman asked a great religious educator, "How early can I begin the religious training of my child?" He replied, "Madam, when will your child be born?" She gasped, "Born! Why, he's already five years old!" "Woman!" he cried, "Don't stand here talking to me! Hurry home, already you've lost the best five years." Some psychologists claim that by the age of three, parents have done more than half of what they will ever do for their child.

Wouldn't it be wonderful if we had the spiritual insight and moral integrity to condition our children for only

the good things in life! They are plastic at our mercy! They not only become like us in action, but they also accept our complexes into their lives as well. A schoolteacher recently asked her class what they thought of the Russians, and they all exclaimed with deep emotional groans of displeasure. She asked them why they did not like the Russians, and they could not give one reason. They had been conditioned to dislike anything connected with Russia.

We all, no doubt, have some ugly "skeletons in our closets." It may be that we don't like Protestants, or Blacks, or Catholics, or Mexicans, or Preachers, or Farmers. This is not because of any intelligent reason, but because we accepted a long time ago the emotional attitudes of our lives in the tender and formative years. The roots go so far back into childhood that we, perhaps, cannot trace them to their source.

The next time Jane or Junior "acts up" in a way that is not good, remember that he or she is a mirror reflecting the action and emotions of his or her elders. Professor James said: "The greatest thing in all education is making our nervous system our ally instead of our enemy." With the help of the Lord, may we be dedicated to the task of giving our children, and those whose lives we influence, the right kind of an example.  Then they will be able to develop a nervous system that will joyfully respond to the real good things in life!

Example Of Parent In Both
Word And Deed Cited

Would you like for your son or daughter to have the best in life? If that is your desire, you have a most worthy ambition, and there is something you can do about it.

Every boy needs a DAD—one worthy of the sublime and exalted title of "Dad." As the young child begins life, his basic need is someone who really loves him. A mature

individual who is interested in him and appreciates him is necessary for his emotional well-being. Then the child can give his love and mold his life after an example that is a pattern worthy of imitating. The child thinks of God as being like Dad. Perhaps your mental picture of God, even today, is colored by your early impressions of your thought of your Dad.

A boy needs an example more than a lecture on an abstract virtue. It is not enough to say, "Son, be a good boy, go to church, read the Bible, etc." That is good advice, but a son is likely to respond something like this, "Who does Dad think he is fooling? If it is not good enough for him, then I don't want it, because I want to be like Dad." This could be applied to every area of life, such as cursing, loafing, gossiping, griping, etc.

The home is the place for the building of a better world. If the home fails, then there is not much chance for the church, school, or state to salvage the lives of children warped by the scourge of prejudice, intolerance, greed, and selfishness.

So, my friend, the responsibility of the rearing of your children is yours. This is a God-given responsibility that cannot be delegated to the church or state or any other agency, and the only way you can give the right impression to your child is to be the right kind of an example, with the right attitudes and complexes and habits.

May we remember these sacred truths as we unconsciously mold the lives of those of our own household. Yes, we can give our children the best in life—a worthy example, in deed and word, in which to mold their lives for the eternal destiny of their souls.

Spiritual Power Seen
As Top Dynamic Force

There is more power in this world than many people realize. Perhaps, the people of this generation are more aware of the physical powers that are dormant, until released, than were the generations before us. This is true because of the discovery of atomic power several generations ago, of space travel, and of all the marvels of computer age. There are many forms of power just waiting to be released, but someone must make the discovery and acquire the skill to unleash them.

We are prone to think that physical powers are more significant and impressive than the less spectacular powers that are known to be in the universe. The sudden jerk of the earthquake and the mighty roar of the sea are, perhaps, thought to be more powerful than the soft rays of the sunshine. However, to the scientific observer the rays of the sunshine are more powerful.

There is also a spiritual power that lies dormant in the hearts of many. This power could be unleashed and made to be a dominant force in the lives of all. The one prerequisite is the desire in the heart of the individual who would receive it. Men of all ages have found this dynamic power. The Bible is a scientific religious manual that tells us of the mighty power of the Eternal Creator, who can charge or regenerate our lives and make them powerful.

The Psalmist realized this power when he wrote: "God is our refuge and strength, a very present help in trouble. Therefore will not we fear thought the earth be removed, and though the mountains be carried into the midst of the sea." Another writer of Holy Writ recognized this potent force in the universe when he said: "He ruleth by his power forever."

The prophet Micah knew that his source of strength was in God, because he said, "I am full of power by the spirit of the Lord." Job even went so far as to say that this eternal power is great enough to lift the soul out of the grave. Job, in his spiritual foresight, said, "I know that my redeemer liveth, and that he shall stand at the latter day upon the earth: and though after my skin worms destroy my body, yet, in my flesh shall I see God."

The secret is found in Jeremiah 29:13, "You will seek me and find when you seek me with all your heart"

Space Age Invokes New Concept Of Stewardship

Many people are thinking today in terms of space travel and staking out claims to the moon and the planets. It makes interesting conversation, and it is wholesome to have open minds to new ideas and enlarging our thoughts. This is indeed an age of new frontiers. However, there are a few basic things that we ought to always remember, whether we are thinking in terms of this world or some heavenly body in space. Many years ago a wise man, through spiritual insight, discovered this fundamental truth: "The earth is the Lord's and the fullness thereof, the world and those who dwell there." That sounds rather all-inclusive, does it not?

This is an interesting thought to elaborate a little about. The world is the Lord's — that is, He still holds title to it. Man sometimes thinks he owns a little of it, but that is only erroneous thinking on his part. It is true that all the natural resources were placed here for man to use for his own benefit, and for him to share with others, but never can man really own the earth! Someone may control a little of the earth and its natural resources for a few years, but this is only a short time in God's viewpoint. Soon man withers like a flower, and someone else arrives to take over.

As we pursue this thought a little farther, we recognize that a man does not even own his life, because his life belongs to the Lord, who created it. It must always be remembered that the Eternal Father reserves the right of life or death over every creature upon the face of the earth. Although our life expectancy has been extended several years by medical science, our houses of dust are still very frail. Our earthly life could be terminated at any time; then, we would have to give an account of our stewardship. It is our responsibility to use that which God has entrusted to us according to His purpose.

The Lord has given man the power to think, and in His word He has said man is to have dominion over His creation. The fulfillment of this idea is coming to pass, more in his day than, perhaps, in any other. Man should extend the boundaries of his life. So, if you want to go to the moon, or one of the planets, best wishes to you for an interesting and worthwhile trip. Just one reminder — all of creation belongs to the Almighty, and someday we will have to make the trip from the Now to the Hereafter. That is the one we need to be more intimately concerned about. Now is the time to make suitable preparation for this imminent journey!

Opportunities

I heard a young man a few days ago complaining about the military service. He thought that everything was working against him. Life was hard. He didn't like his base, the opportunities for promotion were nil, and he didn't make as much money as he would like to make. In other words, he could not see any opportunity for an enriched life. He was defeated.

What has happened to the ring of the liberty bell to many of our young men? Has it lost the challenge that it once had? This day in which we live has many opportunities, if only our eyes could see them.  Most of the world is busy trying to provide enough bread for physical survival and enough clothes and shelter for the bare necessities. This condition is not true in our land. We have plenty of bread to eat — even cake and ice cream; we have plenty of clothes to wear — even pretty colored neckties. Yes, we have everything from an outward appearance to make one happy, but so many times we do not have the inward peace and serenity of mind to be happy and appreciative of the fine things of life.

Our early forefathers were defenders of liberty. They were working for a cause that was much bigger than them; so they were not so much concerned with making a great amount of money and having a high living standard. Their lives were not built around themselves but around the cause of freedom and liberty. Their real security was in the Eternal Father of the Universe. That gave them the eternal security that nothing else could. They worked together with the Giver of Life to carve out a nation dedicated to the principles of righteousness, giving each man his divine right to happiness.

Today we enjoy the fruits of the labors of those who have gone before us. The founders of our nation, under God, gave us a wonderful heritage—both religious and political. May we lift our eyes to the many opportunities for individual development and personal achievement! If the opportunities are not seen, it is not because they are not there. It is just because the vision is dim or nearsighted. Incidentally, life is about the same in the service as out of it. The opportunities are in both places, and very likely persons who cannot see them in one place will not be able to see them in another. On this Independence Day, may we all pause long enough to Thank Our Lord, that we are Americans!

Good Food

Is your soul "run down at the heels?" Do you feel starved for the real spiritual satisfaction that comes from above? Perhaps, we all feel at times that our souls are rather empty and hungry!

To keep our soul filled with the nourishing spiritual food, it is necessary that we daily accept the "bread of life." It would be rather foolish for a person to try to eat enough physical bread to live on for months at a time – in fact, the person who would not accept bread daily would be considered rather strange and in need of medical attention. What about the spiritual application? Is it not rather strange that some people only want spiritual food occasionally?

There are people who go to the garbage cans to seek food, but this is usually when food cannot be procured in  more acceptable ways. It would be strange, indeed, for an individual to prefer the garbage can to the well-set table of delicious foods. There are people, in the world of the spirit, who seem to prefer the garbage can of filth and contamination instead of real wholesome, life-giving spiritual enlightenment.

Maybe it is time for us to make some "down to earth" applications to what I am trying to say. Let us start with the first day of the week, Sunday. Were you interested in going to the Lord's House and seeking to abide in His presence there? Sure, you can find God anywhere, because He is everywhere, but if we are concerned about being in His presence, we will want to honor His day in worship and meditation. You could have gone to church without getting any of the spiritual food, but you were more likely to receive it there. Certainly, physical food can be procured in the fields, but it is easier to pick it up in the commissary or grocery store.

What about the rest of the week? Are you more interested in lurid magazines, filthy picture shows, and smutty conversation, than you are in wholesome magazines, cultural activities, and constructive conversation? If you are more interested in the former than the latter, then you are more interested in eating out of the trash can than the table of spiritual plenty. If you have been surviving by way of the garbage can, look up and receive the food from Him whose desire it is for you to enjoy all good things. If you do, you will find that life can be good and zestful!

Count Your Blessings On
Thanksgiving Day

When Thanksgiving Day rolls around, do we actually use this day to thank God for the many blessings we enjoy? Thanksgiving Day is a national holiday set apart each year for thanksgiving and praising God for His mercies, and there is nothing wrong with remembering Thanksgiving Day throughout the year. It might help us prepare to make the actual day more meaningful. The Pilgrims, many years ago, were exceedingly thankful for their many blessings. They had grain to eat and a place to worship God according to the dictates of their own conscience. Thus they were happy and they did not hesitate to praise God who had provided these blessings for them.

We have made much progress since the early days of our national history. We have so many more things to be thankful for on Thanksgiving Day. We have better clothes to wear. We not only have bread to eat, but we also have cake and ice cream. We not only have a place to worship, but we have comfortable pews. Everything is made for our comfort—and this should add to our happiness. Our dining rooms are carefully screened to keep out insects and nasty flies, our living rooms are lined with lights to drive out the darkness of the evening hours. Most of us have automobiles to take  us anywhere we want to go. Our radio connects us with several radio stations; our telephone links us to our friends all over the world; our computers and the miracle of e-mail and the World Wide Web make communications and commerce instantaneous; and, our TV sets bring the world of entertainment to our reclining couches. The paperboy delivers the news of the world to our doorsteps. Our public libraries have so many books that we can live in most any age of the world's history and with some of the greatest men of the past.

We are living in the most romantic age of the history of mankind. Our nation and our people are blessed above all  other nations and peoples. Even with our blemishes, the United States of America is still the greatest nation on Earth. The Pilgrims had much to be thankful for, but we have so much more! May we use the Thanksgiving Holiday as it was originally intended to be used and really praise God and thank Him for the many, many blessings of life that are given to us to enjoy!

Opportunity for More
Abundant Life Is Ours

There is a story in the Bible about a young lady who pleased the king so much that she was offered a great present. She was given the privilege of asking for a gift—even to half of the king's domain. This must have given her a great thrill to think that she could have almost anything! She immediately went to her mother for advice on such a momentous occasion, as this would be the natural thing for a girl to do. The sad part of the story is that the mother was selfish, and she was more concerned about "getting even" with a certain individual than she was about her daughter's welfare. She wanted the head of a young preacher whose name was John the Baptist. Some of John's words had condemned Herodias as an adulteress, and she was determined to have the head of this preacher some way or another.

The young lady took the advice of her mother and asked for the head of John the Baptist on a platter. The opportunity of a lifetime proved to be a curse rather than a blessing. The difference was because of a harbored grudge. This looks absurd, does it not? How often have we been guilty of similar foolish mistakes?

God has offered to us more than half an earthly ruler's kingdom! He has offered us eternal life and the peace of mind that comes with a repentant heart. Have we been more interested in "John's head?" As sure as light and darkness are opposites, so are love and hatred. It is impossible for a person to harbor ill will in his heart against another person and have the love of God that gives peace of mind. You may have one, but never can you have both. If your mind has been filled with resentment and grudges, with the grace of God you can change your way of thinking and accept the way of love and peace. The opportunity of a more abundant life is knocking at your door. You may or may not open it—that is your choice.

Man Breaks Man's Laws;
God's Are Unbreakable

There are moral laws as well as physical laws that cannot be broken. Man often breaks man's laws, and it is often said that man breaks God's laws, but God's laws are unbreakable, because they are eternal.

The person who tries to break God's law of gravity by climbing a 15 story building and jumping out the window will be crushed and physically destroyed by that law. He does not break the law, the law breaks him.

God's moral laws are just as immutable as his physical laws, but perhaps they are not so self-evident. There is the law of love. This gives the individual peace and joy. The person who observes this law can live in harmony with God, himself, and the rest in society. Forgiveness is the law of love in action. We have no right to ask for forgiveness unless we forgive others. In fact, God cannot forgive an unforgiving heart, because to do so would be reversing the moral law of love.

It is spiritual suicide to try to break the moral laws of the universe — they always backfire!

Some people talk about freedom as if it meant that we were free to disregard the moral law. They seem to think that the Lord of the Universe is a tough police cop, seeking to catch a culprit. The true picture would be more like a sympathetic physician, prescribing a remedy that will cure. However, if we will not let Him be the latter, He may become the former.

The spiritual laws may work slower, but they "grind exceedingly small." If there is a doubt in your mind, it might be well for you to re-study the moral law and re-evaluate your life. You might begin by reading Exodus 20. Then, read John 13:34 and Romans 13:8-10. If there is still a doubt, you might look up the finality of breaking the moral law of God (Romans 6:23).

It is so easy to jump at conclusions. The man who jumps from the window of a 15 story building might pass the 14th and 13th stories saying, "This is a thrill!" So it is with the man who disregards God's moral law, but the crash is as sure to come. Are you building your future upon moral implications? If not, now is the time to do some sober thinking!

Easter Message Is Same
Today As Centuries Ago

Easter Season is here again. We will the thinking about how awful the people were who crucified Jesus on the cruel cross of Calvary, but are we any different today? It does us very little good to think about the evils of the people of another generation unless it is an incentive for us to do better. It is easy for us to pass judgment on others, but when we are emotionally involved in a social or religious atmosphere it is harder for us to be objective in our own conduct.

The Easter Message is as relevant today as it was twenty centuries ago. People are about the same today as they were then. Most everyone is interested in the message of the empty tomb, because man has an unquenchable thirst for fellowship with God and the hope of immortality. Most all the Christian churches will be presenting the message of the cross as we approach the Easter services. However, there will be only the faithful few who will be interested in hearing about the cross, because that indicates the responsibilities of the Christian life.

If we can judge this year by the past, the churches on Easter Sunday will be filled. This is one time in the year that most of the churches will only have standing room. This is indicative of the fact that people are more interested in the privileges of the gospel rather than the responsibilities. Some fail to realize that the privileges only come after the individual has taken up HIS cross. Easter came, and comes today, only to those who were and are willing to accept the Christian cross. On that first Easter morning Jesus appeared to His disciples. Those individuals who nailed Him to the cross did not know about the wonderful reality of the resurrection. The cross is still "foolishness to those who are perishing."

Are you preparing for Easter, or do you plan on driving some more nails into the cross? This can be the "season of all seasons" if you prepare for it. But it will mean nothing to you unless you do. Don't plan on an hour's Easter service giving you a new hope. But make spiritual preparation in all the days leading up to it by divesting your minds of all evil and frivolity; and, with faith in the resurrected Christ, your life can be renovated by the sweet morsels of the truth of the Easter message that can last a lifetime!

Joy Of Worship Makes
Life Sweet, Wonderful

Life is so sweet and wonderful to those who have learned the joy of worship. It is through real worship that we squeeze out those things in our lives that cause fears and frustration. The coming into the presence of the Holy God means that we have left on the outside all feelings of bitterness, envy, and falsehood.

It is in worship that we learn to live in the present, abiding in the spirit of the Eternal. It is then possible for us to replace fear with faith. The temporal fears are seen in eternal perception, reducing them to a minimum, and life is seen as an Eternal Existence — giving life the anchors in which to establish a permanent stability. Therefore, life can be like a clock ticking through a thunderstorm at its normal beat.

Peace is the result of vital worship. When we are in harmony with God, we have no hate for others, because God is Love, and we live in love when we abide in His presence. We have no bitterness, because in worship we have to become big enough to appreciate the wonderful blessings of life, instead of having shriveled-up hearts that can only grow when their egos have been inflated by the petty experiences of day-to-day living.

There is another joy of worship in the form of service. The spiritual axiom of "it is more blessed to give than to receive" is true to the person who has known the joy of worship.

So it is that worship of God is the greatest privilege that man can experience. It is through this experience that man can find himself and can make peace with God and self. This is truly the most joyous of all activities. If this is not your experience, then come to Him and enjoy the blessings of Eternal Life.

The Key To Peace Is Within Everyone

Peace is a word that is used often. It expresses the desire of the peoples of the world. We all wish for a time when all nations would "beat their swords into plowshares." This would indicate a mutual love, trust, and respect between the nations, creeds, and nationalities. This is a goal that each of us ought to be personally interest in.

The world is big, with millions of peoples, and our voice is usually lost in the cry of the masses. We do, however, have a realm of influence, and we ought to be interested in doing something of permanent good in this realm.

The most significant achievement for each of us is within our own soul or self. Unless we conquer in this citadel, we will likely fail in all others. To conquer here is to have the peace of mind that goes beyond human understanding. It is the peace that permits a person to enjoy living with himself. He realizes that he has stood for what he believed to be truth and goodness. He has accepted in his life an abstract God, which has given him the ability to accept himself. He has surrendered all his will, hatred, and greed to his Maker and has received in return good will, love, and kindness, which gives peace to the human soul.

Do you have this peace? It can be yours! If all the individuals of the world had this peace, the world could live without war and strife. So, may we start and make over the world, and begin with ourselves!

Inventory Of Personal Life
Leads To Victory

What do you want from the year 2002? Each year, usually somewhere around the first of the year, but anytime will do, many people take an inventory of their assets and liabilities. Retailers and car dealerships take inventory each year so that they can intelligently plan for the year ahead.

There is another inventory that should concern each of us. That is the inventory of our personal lives. What are our assets and liabilities? In April of each year we figure our income tax—but there is another system of assets and liabilities that cannot be figured in terms of dollars and cents. What about our physical appearance? Do we have an extra "flab" of flesh around the waistline? Do we feel "run down at the heels," or do we have a "spring in our step?" What about our friends? Do we have a good selection of them? Are we seeking new ones and conserving the old? Then there are those ever-present habits that control us from morning to night. We have physical, mental, and spiritual habits that become our master. What about those attitudes and complexes? Do we greet the newborn world with a smile everyday, or do we face it with a "chip on our shoulders" — daring someone to knock it off?

After we have made this inventory, then what shall we do? Our attitude might be, "I am what I am and I do not expect nor desire to be any better or any worse." Of course, the person with that attitude is selling out too cheap, because there is much in the realm of personality development for each of us, if we will only strive to find it.

After we have made an inventory and evaluation of our lives, then it is time to make some constructive decisions and preparation for a change. We must go forward, or we shall go backward. The earth is in constant motion; the solar system is never motionless. Time is moving forward always, and we can never stop it for a moment. So this year will move forward, and at the end of it we will be one year nearer the grave. If we neglect to make our lives better by the changing of our habits, attitudes, and complexes, then we will have only been marking time; and, the very purpose of time will have been defeated for our personal lives. This year can be the best in our lives, or it can be the worst. The determining factor is within our reach. With faith in God and the assurance of an eternal career, we can rise above all the roadblocks of the year and come through to the end with blessings of spiritual victory!

Aesop's Fables Still Contain
Valuable Lessons For Today

Aesop was a Greek slave who lived in the 6th century B.C. He was a great teacher; however, he did not have a title, nor did he have a book from which to teach. His audience usually consisted of a few children. There was much selfishness and greed in his day, as there has been in every other age. He taught much against evil—but in a very subtle way. His tools were various animals, such as frogs, mice, grasshoppers, birds, wolves, dogs, etc. His speaker's platform was on a hillside somewhere in ancient Greece. Aesop could be called the " Father of Fables."

Did you ever hear Aesop's fable of the "The Dog and His Shadow?" This fable is about a dog that was crossing a smooth, clear stream by means of a plank. The dog had in his mouth a large piece of meat that he had stolen. Looking in the stream, he saw what he thought was another dog carrying a piece of meat. He snapped greedily at his shadow, thinking that he might get the other portion also. However, when he opened his mouth, the meat fell down, down, far into the stream, and the greedy dog never saw it again.

Now isn't that the way of a great number of people today? They are never satisfied with what they have, and they are always snapping at the other person and trying to get what he has. We can usually detect this abominable characteristic in other people, but do we ever think about looking for it in our own personality? We have many mottos and expressions that indicate the same truth that Aesop was trying to present. Such sayings as, "Live and Let Live," "Do Unto Others as You Would Have Them Do Unto You," and "Living for Others" suggest a better way of life than Aesop's dog. May we evaluate our life, and if it is filled with greed, may we seek to change our way of life and live for others.

Self Evaluation Is Key
To Well-Balanced Life

Could you give me a good evaluation of self? Are you acquainted with yourself? Do you know how you would react under various conditions in life? Suppose you were given the world to rule, as was young Alexander, would you still act like a gentleman? Suppose the doctor broke the news to you that you only had a few months to live, would you live them in trust and humility? It is easy for us to criticize the other person for the way he plays the game of life. It is easy for us to sit on the sideline and see the mistakes of the players, but if the play was ours, would we do any better? We are prone to criticize our neighbor for throwing foul balls, but do we always put them over the plate?

A hard person to get acquainted with is this fellow "Self." Here are a few suggestions how we can know him a little better. We can look backward and see what he has done in the past. We can note his reaction when asked to do the difficult job, the unusual task, or his reaction when confronted with some subtle temptation. When he was behind, did he complain about the fellow ahead of him? Did Self accuse him of running on a foul ball? Did he throw a stumbling block in the way of the runner so he would trip and fall?

In this study of personal integrity, it is also revealing to note how Self acted when he got ahead. Did it puff up his ego? Did it make him boast how great he was and how stupid the fellow behind him was? Would he "strut standing still" as some are capable of doing? Or, did success give Self a sense of gratitude and humility? If we look at our past with an open mind, perhaps we can all see some weak places that could be made stronger.

Another way to get better acquainted with Self is to give an unprejudiced evaluation of his present status quo. How high is his moral standard, and what mood does he usually live in? Is old Self pretty hard to get along with? Does he complain, grumble, and gripe when he is not in the limelight? Does he condemn the person who is less religious than he by saying that he is an evil person? Does he condemn the person who is more religious than he by saying that he is an extremist? Or, is Self always compassionate and understanding?

Let us forever be at the task of getting a better understanding of Self! Then, if we only try, we have a good chance to improve. If we will spend more time trying to understand our faults and failures and how to overcome them, and less time trying to understand the other fellow and his faults and failures, then we will be on the road to a greater life. Someone has said, "the greatest room in the world is room for improvement." This being true, may we enter into a life that is more abundant and complete!

Many Prefer Being A Religious Spectator

A spectator is one who stands on the sideline and watches the players participating in the game. He usually has a team picked to win. That makes the game more exciting.

The spectator cheers the team of this choice when they are wining. When his team is behind, he may yell at the umpire or call the players of the opposing team abusive names. If his team falls way behind, he may begin ridiculing his own team. If this happens very much, he may decide to change teams, because he certainly wants to be on the side of the winner.

Life is like that. Some are in the game – doing their best; others are not so good; and, the great majority is on the sideline observing the players. This application could be made in many areas of life—politics, education, economics, and religion. May we make one final observation in this area of religion?

The religious spectator comes to church when he thinks the activity to be interesting. The minister, the choir, the ushers, and other attendants have everything prepared for his comfort and interest. He will, perhaps, be glad to pay his quarter as an admission fee when the ticket man passes the plate. If the game goes like he wants it to, he may be thrilled, and he may even come back for another performance. When asked to participate in the program of the church, he always has his answer. It may be in many pious platitudes like, "others can play better," or "I am too busy," but, actually he is just saying, "No, thank you, I just prefer to be a Spectator and watch the game from the bleachers."

Watch Those Thoughts

We read in the Good Book that "whatsoever a man thinketh in his heart, so is he." So that would lead us to believe that our thoughts are very important. It is not our education that is of supreme worth, but it is our thoughts that give us worth and eternal blessings!

If thoughts are all that important, we should be very diligent to guard the chamber of our minds. So we need to drain out the trash in our minds and keep those thoughts that are worthy and uplifting. Some of the trash to flush out are lusts, anger, hostility, grudges, depression, and covetousness. Books could be written about each of those negative thought patterns, but let us zero in on the idea of hostility. That usually happens when we are wronged or when we think we have been wronged. There could be lots of reasons that a person _thinks_ he has been wronged, and harbors hostility. Maybe someone stole his girlfriend, or someone talked about him, or maybe he did not get his fair share of the family inheritance.

What does hostility do to the person who harbors it? Other synonyms that describe that state of being are anger, wrath, and grudge. Oftentimes, depression accompanies it. A person can become obsessed with the thoughts of hostility so much that it becomes impossible for that person to dwell in the sunshine of God's grace.

People sometimes carry hostility in the form of grudges all the way to the grave. Suppose one's parents died, and the heirs were left with hundreds of acres of land. The inheritance was divided, but in the process, three of the boys were left with bad relations — Two against one. They lived long lives just a few miles apart, but they never associated with one another. When one of the three died, a neighbor went to get one of them to take him to the funeral, but he refused to go. Eventually, they all died and were buried side by side in the family plot in the cemetery. I knew such a family and have visited their graves many times, and each time, the thought comes to me, "They could not live together in life, but now that are side by side—what a tragedy!"

Do you have hostility in your heart? It so, it needs to be removed! It is a plague that can destroy the soul. Remember that vengeance belongs to God, who is just and who knows all the facts. Let Him flush out the trash so He can give you a heart of forgiveness, love, and compassion. Then you can think good thoughts, because it is true that "whatsoever a man thinketh in his heart, so is he!" (Proverbs 23:7)

Past Experience Should
Help In Building For Future

Life is a series of events. Each day should be a building block for another day of progressive brightness and character maturity. Each decade in life brings new experiences and personal ambitions. Each can be more exciting and interesting to the individual whose spiritual life grows and matures with the passing of the years. When we move onward in progress and upward, in reach of the Eternal, we can see new heights to ascend, new horizons to approach; and, a deeper life of serenity and gratitude can be ours to enjoy. This is the unfolding of life and it should be the experience of us all.

Two men were talking about people and the past. One said, "Ole Si just ain't what he used to be!" The other said, "No, nor he never was!" We usually look at the past, not as it was, but as we would have liked for it to have been. The individual who has nothing but the past to look at is a maladjusted person. We can't live in the past – it is gone forever.

The past can be used to build for the future. There are sweet memories to recall; there are great lessons of inestimable worth. It is exciting to think of the past with the old covered wagons traveling westward seeking new and unexplored lands. These pictures can be wholesome in our world of imagination. However, to want to go back to that day is another thing. Time goes on! To go backward makes no sense, either in the earthly here and now or in the Christian's walk. To go backward in the development of a fulfilling life is not what God has in mind for His People! We should make it our goal each and every day to make this day that the Lord has made just a little bit better than the day before. If we want to FULLY maximize our Christian walk, our outward focus should be to make each day better. When

Jesus walked the Earth more than 2,000 years ago, His entire focus was on others' needs. He was totally engrossed in helping others in their earthly needs and in their spiritual fulfillment.

Looking back to past failures and regrets or relying on past successes to guide you through life is simply not healthy, spiritually or physically. Focus on making tomorrow the best it can be in God's eye, and you won't be sorry, for eternity!

Man Must Prepare For
Eternal Career Today

Immortal means imperishable, eternal, or everlasting. We speak of men whose fame is immortal, but the idea of immortality of the soul is more personal to each of us. The hope of an everlasting existence is real in the minds of all peoples of the world. Without this truth of immortality, everything is doomed for failure.

Physical and tangible things are insecure and perishable. Man has learned many of the secrets of the Universe. He is capable of releasing enough energy to physically destroy a large city in only a very short interval of time. Perhaps, we have been made more aware in recent times of the insecurity of material things, especially with the events of 9/11. Our physical bodies are tangible and visible; but, our real selves are invisible to the human eye. No man has seen God at any time; neither has the spirit of man been seen by man. Our bodies are only vehicles for us to ride, and this implies the idea of limitation. At death, the body dies, but the individual continues to exist as a real person.

A wise man centuries ago asked the question: "If a man dies will he live again?" Centuries later the question was answered by Jesus of Nazareth. He not only taught the idea of immortality, but he demonstrated it. Jesus put much emphasis on the importance of the soul of man. In fact, he said that the soul of one man was worth more than the entire physical world. This in not true of the physical body of man; but it is true because man is both spiritual and eternal.

Jesus was crucified and buried in a tomb which was sealed and guarded by Roman soldiers. There was no cross that could kill the spirit of Jesus; there was no power that could keep him in a tomb. On the third day he arose from the tomb and demonstrated to the world that man lives beyond the grave.

My friend, do you realize that you are an immortal soul, and that your soul is more important than the entire world? This life is a time for eternal preparation, so may we get busy on our eternal career and prepare ourselves for great things in the immortal future.

Man's Search For God
Seen In All Of History

"Can an intelligent person believe in a personal God?" is a question that some have asked in every generation.

Man has looked through the microscope with his physical eyes and has not been able to find God; he has scanned the heavens with the telescope and has not seen His image; he has searched the pages of history unable to find conclusive proof in the reality of God; and, the surgeon has cut open the heart of man and has not found God there.

Other men have looked through the microscope and have declared that only an intelligent Creator could have arranged the tiny molecules in such a meticulous manner. Some have pointed their telescopes skyward and looked millions of light years away and, overwhelmed with the idea of the order of astronomical bodies, concluded that only an omnipotent God could perform such a majestic feat. Many historians have believed that they could see the hand of God in the development of history. They have noted that every nation that has outlawed god has gone down in oblivion.

"But there are some brilliant minds who do not believe in the existence of God!" Perhaps. One great fallacy of the age is to accept a man to be an authority by the degrees attached to his name. This is an age of specialization, and a specialist in one field of study may be ignorant in another. The mathematician may know very little about psychology; and, the chemist may know nothing in the technological field of aviation. Neither is it surprising to find some educated men in fields of specialized learning to be ignorant of the fundamental laws of the Kingdom of God. On the other hand, there are men of spiritual insight from every field of advanced education. To not admit this would be to parade one's ignorance or prejudice, or both. Dr. Moon of the Moody Institute of Science testifies to the fact that God is real because

he dwells within his heart. President Bush pleads with the nation to put God first in their lives, because he knows that it is only by the power of God that our nation can survive. Albert Einstein in "Scientific Truth" said: "A conviction akin...to religious feeling, of the rationality or intelligibility of the world lies behind all scientific work of a higher order. This firm belief in a superior mind that reveals itself in the world of experience represents my concept of God."

Yes, intelligent men can believe in a personal God, and their lives can never be in peace with themselves until they have become in harmony with God. "Ask, and it shall be given you; seek, and ye shall find; knock, and it shall be opened unto you." It can be a science only revealed to those who have this experimental knowledge. If you are really interested in knowing about the reality of a personal God, ask a person who daily walks with Him, because he is the only authority in the field of religion. "Those that seek me early shall find me." (Proverbs 8:17b)

Living A Godly Life Calls
For Godly Reasoning

A young man told me a little while ago that he didn't go to church because there were hypocrites in the church; yet he was so irresponsible that he was in the process of breaking up another man's family by stealing the affection of his wife. This same fellow said that he didn't believe in getting drunk on Saturday night and going to church on Sunday; yet, he exhibited the odor of a brewery. He was certain that if, and when, he became a Christian, he would really "walk the chalk line."

The above line of "reasoning" is what psychologists call rationalization. It actually has no logical reason to it. This tissue paper barricade is easy to see through. He first did what he wanted to do—being led by the flesh rather than the spirit - then he sought for a plausible explanation. He wanted to live a profligate life, and his greatest hindrance was his conscience and God's moral law.

If he could convince himself that the church—which to him was a symbol of moral law—was no good and that the ones who went to church were hypocrites, then he could convince himself that he was just as good as they. Therefore, he didn't need to go to church. However, he still wanted to hold on to a little ray of hope for an eternal future; sometime, somewhere, "I will change my life, and I am the kind of a fellow that does what he says he will do."

The fallacy of this man's "thinking" is that he is not thinking; he is only rationalizing. The Bible indicates that those who become like the Father, God, do it gradually. They "grow in the grace of God." When they accept the principles of the kingdom of God, they are "babes in Christ." That is, the path to character and integrity is a gradual growth process. Seldom does a person leap from the lowest pit in hell to the highest pedestal in heaven.

Yes, my friend, your ambition to become one of the most honorable and best of the children of men is a worthy endeavor; but if you wish to accomplish this, the best advice I know is to start where you are and walk in the right direction. When you do, you will see that the chasm was too much for one big leap.

Opportunity Seen With
Growth In Grace Of God

Growth is the assimilation of new matter into a living organism, either plant or animal life. Flowers are interesting to watch as they grow and develop into beautiful flowers in bloom. We like to watch children as they grow from the cradle into adulthood. We like to watch them develop both physically and mentally, and we become alarmed if they do not develop properly.

It is our opportunity as God's children to grow another way. We can grow in the grace of God and in the knowledge of Eternal things. It is in this way that we can better prepare ourselves to meet life with its sorrows and joys, and its defeats and victories.

God is not willing that any should perish; neither is he willing that any should enter the other world as little souls. When we reach the other side, all chances of spiritual growth may be terminated. Now is the time to grow spiritually. Would you like to spend an eternity with a spirit of animosity toward someone, or a grudge, or with an unforgiving spirit? If your mental attitude is not good, it is your privilege, with the help of the Almighty, to change it.

Our spiritual Father knew that man was weak and that he would pass up most of his everyday opportunities to advance spiritually, so he provided other means. Sometimes it is necessary that God take material wealth from a person and cast him into extreme poverty before he realizes his need for the Creator. Others realize their need for God when they are on the sickbed of affliction. The Psalmist may have had this in mind when he said: "It is good for me that I have been afflicted."

All trails and burdens that you overcome will make you stronger than before. If a burden or trouble leaves us with a kinder heart and more helpful to our fellow men, we dare not call it disaster, no matter how horrible it may appear on the surface.

God's ways are not man's ways. Perhaps, if we used all the everyday opportunities we have for spiritual advancement, God would not need to use painful experiences to lead us into a more consecrated walk with Him. It is God's will that we grow spiritually. So may we use every opportunity that comes our way to become bigger and more spiritually in tune.

Power Of Good Thought
Determines Character

What are you thinking about? Are you thinking about a new trick for a "crap" game? ...How to get even with some "wise guy" who did you dirty? ...or, are you thinking about some way to make the world a better place in which to live?

What we do today is perhaps the result of what we were thinking about yesterday, and what we do tomorrow will be determined by our meditations today. Therefore, it is very important that we think good thoughts. A person's thoughts are so important that a very wise man, Marcus Aurelius, once said, "A man's life is what his thoughts make of him."

You may be saying, "That sounds good, but I have too many troubles and worries to practice thinking good thoughts." However, the fact is, many have been able to rise above the most adverse circumstances of life and have been able to think good thoughts in the midst of evil.

Paul, of the New Testament Scriptures, was able to rejoice and be happy while tied to a ball and chain and guarded by a Roman soldier. He was happy because he had learned the lesson of pure Thought. Many had done Paul wrong, and he had suffered many injustices, but he spent his time thinking about the good things of life, rather than trying to get even with the world.

So, may we think good thoughts today and forget those grudges and evil thoughts, because thoughts are so powerful that they determine our actions and mold our character. Therefore, to be a noble character, it is imperative that we practice the art of thinking good thoughts. May this be our life-long project for our everyday living! Our reward will be great! "Blessed are the pure in heart, for they shall see God." (Matthew 5:8)

Prayer Gives Feeling
Of Deep Understanding

The key to the heart of God is prayer, and prayer is talking to God. It is a two-way conversation, but it is not necessarily audible—it is a feeling of compassionate understanding.

Different people pray for different things. Some are worthy prayers and some are unworthy. It is sheer nonsense to waste your time and God's time in asking for a mere million dollars when you could be asking for more of the spirit of God, which is vastly more important.

There are some wrong conceptions of prayer. Prayer is not so much trying to change the mind of God as it is finding the mind or will of God for one's life. It is true that "prayer changes things," but it is usually more accurate to say that prayer changes me.

We understand through prayerful fellowship with the Divine that every experience of life can be used to make us bigger and more mature in character. It gives us the answers for the difficult questions in life.

One of the hard questions in life is: "Why should a godly man suffer?" It is easy for most of us to see that suffering, in many instances, is the direct result of evil. For instance, the drunken driver or the overbearing bully causes much suffering. Our highways are present-day battlefields that cause much suffering. It is folly to say that this is the will of God. Yet, even in this kind of suffering, God is sometimes blamed for it.

The Bible tells us about two men who suffered greatly—Job and Paul. Job lived in the early history of mankind. In his day the people believed that every event came immediately from the hand of God; prosperity indicated the favor of God, and calamity indicated the anger of God. Job was a rich man "with all the trimmings," so he was acclaimed to be righteous before God. When his wealth, health, and family were taken from him, his friends accused him of evil. He had a time (perhaps one year) of intense suffering. It was through prayer that Job was able to see the hand of God pointing to a greater life of spiritual maturity. He saw that this particular time of suffering was to prove to the world that a godly man serves God for a higher motive than just wealth, health, or protection for his loved ones.

Paul had a "thorn in the flesh." He prayed earnestly that God remove it. Each time Paul prayed about this, the answer came back, "My grace is sufficient for you." So Paul learned to live with the thorn in the flesh and to go rejoicing each day living in the sunshine of his grace.

Spiritual 'Suicide' Is Danger To Many Others

"It is nobody's business whether I go to church or not! This is a free country and we are free to do what we want to, so why make a fuss about going to church?" This seems to be an attitude that is not foreign to some.

With your permission, may we pursue this thought into other areas of life? Such as, "It is none of the doctor's business whether I abide by the rules of sanitation and good health, or not. This is a free country and I ought to be able to jump into the swimming pool with a sore on my arm if I want to. After all, it is my arm and it is my sore!" Or, would we say, "It is none of the judge's business whether I drive 40 miles an hour or 85 miles an hour. It is my car—and if I am risking my life, that is my business!"

Do I hear someone say that the thoughts are not relevant, because they are not closely related? Certainly a person ought not go swimming with a sore, because that would contaminate the pool for everyone else! True, but what about contaminating the pool of community thought by hypocrisy and irreligion? But I thought all the hypocrites went to church. No, a hypocrite is a person who claims to be religious and lives otherwise. So the person who claims to be a Christian (and most people do) can fall in this category, whether he goes to church or not. If you had the seeds of a pestilence in your body, you would not have a more active contagion than you have in your attitude of frivolity and irreligion. This is an unconscious influence! It is not just a matter of your own spiritual suicide, but everyone you meet is in immediate danger.

The doctor has a "club" that he might wield by issuing a directive to prohibit action in medical areas you ought not go. The judge has another, impressive "club," in which he can use by demanding, "A hundred dollars please!" The preacher or pastor has a different kind of "club," which is the appeal to the God-given ability of man to reason. This becomes the most effective club of all to those who will listen to the "still small voice" that is not completely silenced.

An intelligent man would not live with his family if he knew he had a dreaded contagious disease; a wise person would not drive recklessly down the highway with his family in the car; a thoughtful man should realize that his prayerful attitude and faithful attendance to the church of his choice makes an eternal impression on his family and friends.

This matter of spiritual activities becomes the interest of all who are interested in a well-ordered society and in making sensible preparation for an eternal career in the home that is not too far in the future for any of us! Then shall the King say unto them on his right hand, "Come, ye blessed of my Father, inherit the kingdom prepared for you from the foundation of the world." (Matt. 25:34)

Weapon To Stop Spread Of
Communism And Terrorism Is Basic

I had an unusual dream a few nights ago; the American people had come to a place in the history of the nation where they were questioning the principles of the Constitution of the United States and our way of life. Many had accepted the principles of Communism, and most of the other people seemed to be indifferent to ethics and philosophy. I had a peculiar feeling. It was only for a moment and I was awake again, but the thought still lingers with me. Could this be the state of the nation in some future time? Are there too many people even today without real eternal convictions by which to live?

The worldwide struggles of Communism, terrorism, and despotic dictatorships with the West is a struggle between ideologies. Basically it is not who can make the biggest bomb or the fastest missile, but who can sell their ideology first to the uncommitted part of the world. Not only are the neutral nations the target, but there are infiltrators in all parts of the world trying to convince the world that Communism, and now terrorism, is the best for the people. We have been less diligent to advance the principles of freedom.

Communism and terrorism are international systems. There are men from every nationality that have convinced themselves that joining up with Communism is good. In doing this they have given up all former codes of ethics or behavior. The influence and spread of terrorism is becoming painfully obvious since 9/11. It is hard to believe that intelligent men could sell their freedom for Communism, terrorism, and the other horrors of despotism, but it is true.

Communism appeals more to the emotions than the rational thought of the minds of men. The same is true of terrorism, even though terrorism does not necessarily equal

Communism, nor vice versa. They are sold on the idea that here is a cause that is big, and it is a basic hunger to be identified with something stronger than self. Communism and terrorism pretend to fight against misery, poverty, and injustice. This is evil. They pretend to fight for justice, equality, and peace. This is good. Therefore they have convinced themselves that they are fighting against evil and for good. Their key personnel are dedicated men and women. That is, they are people who are willing to sacrifice their lives for their ideology. This is especially true with the recent horrors of terrorism of 9/11 and other instances around the globe. Lenin demanded that those who followed him must give their lives—not just part of them—for the cause of Communism. Strange as it may seem, his followers have made great impact on the globe and still have strong pockets in such places as Castro's Cuba.

What do we have that can stop this spread of Communisms and terrorism? A negative approach is not enough; neither is a budget of billions for implements for war, even though the current war on terrorism seems to be a reasonable immediate reaction to the problem, given the circumstances. War is not a permanent fix. We do have the effective weapons for the task. They are found in our Christian ideology and in the Constitution of the United States. Our forefathers gave us the weapons. It is our task to use them. Are we willing to apply the principles of the moral law to our everyday lives and to be dedicated to the task of making the world a better place in which to live? The task is big and the responsibility is great, but with the help of Eternal Providence we can do it!

Seeking For The Chief Good

The American people like the best in everything. They like the best in clothes, food, cars, and everything of a material nature. However, it is often true that we are not as interested in having the best of the eternal thing in life. Often we are satisfied with cheap things in this realm.

What are the best things in life and what is the chief good of the all? Can life's best be found in the accumulation of things? Jesus tells about a man who laid up much wealth for the future (Luke 12:13-21). His barns were full and running over and yet God called him a fool, because he neglected to fill his life with the best. He satisfied his animal nature but neglected that part of himself that was made in the image of God. He had prepared enough for his donkey, but that was not enough to satisfy the hunger and thirst of man. Therefore, the Master said, "Take heed, and beware of covetousness: for a man's life consisteth not in the abundance of the things which he possesseth (v. 19).

One man (Ecclesiastes 2) tried the way of "Wine, Women and Song" in his search for the chief good. He said, "I sought in mine heart to give myself unto wine," and again, "I got me servants and maidens," and finally he said, "I got me men singers and woman singers, and the delights of the sons of men." After he had given himself to folly, his conclusion was: "Wisdom excelleth folly as far as light excelleth darkness."

Where then can the chief good in life be found? It is not to be found in things, nor in sensual living. In words of scripture the conclusion of the whole matter is, "Fear God, and keep His commandments: for this is the whole duty of man." Therefore, the best in life is to be measured in terms of eternal values rather than the temporal; it is to be measured in terms of the spiritual rather than the sensual. Thus, may we resolve in our hearts to live for the eternal rather than the temporal; may we be more interested in filling our souls than in filling our barns.

My Dad's Razor Strap

Pa (that was the name I had for my Dad) used to shave his beard each Sunday morning before we went to church. We lived in a three-roomed house with a front porch and a back porch that circled around the north room. The front porch was facing south, and there was a big trunk in the living room. That is where he kept his butcher knife, razor, razor strap, and a mug with a brush and soap in it. The razor strap consisted of two pieces of leather about 2 inches wide and about 18 inches long. When he went to get his shaving equipment, there was a big thud when he lifted and lowered the lid of the trunk. He would strap the razor, put water in the mug, and go out to the front porch to shave.

I never shall forget about what happened one Sunday morning. Pa was not a teacher. He did not have a college education—not even high school. So he had never studied Psychology or Sociology, nor had he received any formal training on how to rear children; but, he taught me a lesson that day that was one of the most impressive lessons I have ever learned. Our church was a small congregation and we met in a one-room building in the Winn Hill Community, which had a cemetery, a school, a church, and a mailbox. It was about a mile and a half from our house. We went to church in our Model T Ford.

While we were in church that morning, I was having fun with my mother. She tried to corral me, but I was having too much fun to be serious. I was really not very interested in what the preacher was saying, anyway. I remember sliding down the long pew bench, and she would slide after me. Then I would get on the other side and slide the other way. It was a fun time.

After church, we got in the car and Pa drove home. Everything was very quiet as we rode home. But some how I sensed that something was wrong. Pa just wasn't acting the way I thought that he should. So, when the car stopped in front of our house, I made a beeline for the east side of our house where it was underpinned with a row of stones. Some of the stones were missing, so I knew that I could crawl under the house. So that is what I did, thinking that I could weather the storm.

When Pa got out of the car, he went to the big trunk. By that time, I was under the floor of that room, so I could hear the thud of the lid, and I knew that it was bad news. Pa was a man of few words, and the only words that I remember him saying that day was when he looked under the floor were, "Clyde, come out from under there." His voice was not loud, but it was commanding, and I knew that Judgment Day had arrived. I crawled out like a person facing a firing squad, and I met Pa with that razor strap in his hand. He had already shaved, so I knew that he did not need it to whet his razor. He used it that day for a far nobler service.

I did not give my parents any trouble the next Sunday, or the next, or the next—in fact, that was a lesson that made an indelible impression on me. So Pa did turn out to be a great teacher, and I shall always be grateful to him for his concept of eternal values that really make life precious and wonderful.

Daily Fellowship With
God Solves Problems

Have you ever had a problem in your life that you did not know how to solve? If you have not had such a problem, you are quite unusual. Certainly, just around the corner there will be one—for there are many occasions in life that are too big for us to handle. We must face life with all of its complexities; and we constantly encounter the possibilities of death and eternity. In the course of our lives we, perhaps, are perplexed with the many mysteries of the universe. We may be struggling with moral and philosophical questions too big for our small minds to comprehend. So, my friend, it is rather important to be on speaking terms with our Creator.

Some people have the idea that God is not needed unless they are in trouble. They are like the old sea dog who had spent years at sea. The storm was raging and it looked as if the old ship was going to capsize any minute. There had been other critical moments in the old sailor's life, but not like this time. It looked as if the end was near. Any moment might be the last one as far as this side of eternity was concerned. So, for the first time in his life he fell down on his knees and began praying. His prayer went something like this: "Lord, I have lived a long time and I have been able to get along alright without you, but I am now in quite a predicament. So I would very much like your help at this time. I have never bothered you before, and if you will get me out of this mess, I will never bother you again!" Is not that the way of many people today? They do not think of calling upon the Eternal until the chips are down.

The Lord of Creation is also the Father of mankind. He would like to be an everyday companion. If you desire His presence, He will abide with you. It is not necessary to call loud and long to be heard by the Almighty, but if you will open the door of your heart, He will communicate with you.

You can find in Him the answer to your problem, regardless of how complicated it may be. He would also like to fellowship with you daily to make life more exciting and joyful.

Atmosphere Of Church
Seen As 'Penetrating'

You may be saying, "I can worship God in bed, so why should I go to church?" It is true that you can worship God at home as well as you can learn typing or history at home, but the atmosphere is more conducive to learning in a study room or classroom rather than in bed. The power of influence is great and we have a tendency to act like the people we are around.

At church the congregation sings, "This is My Father's World," and we join in singing at least part of it. We may also join in singing with the congregation, "Take My Life, and Let it Be." These songs may first start with the lips, but the words have a tendency of moving downward until they have penetrated the heart. We are truly a part of all "we have ever met," so it is important that we come in contact with the good in life, if we want that to become a part of us.

Some may object saying, "There are hypocrites in the church!" That fact is assumed without argument, but do you not find them at the bar, the movie, and in the restaurant? Why should you be so surprised to find them at church? When Jesus organized His church, Judas was with them. The other 11 disciples did not refuse to follow Jesus just because Judas was along. When we become more interested in our own self-improvement and advance in spiritual enlightenment, it may be revealed to us that the person whom we thought to be a hypocrite was just a weak person, just as we are.

Carnegie says that there are two reasons why we do things. One reason is the one that sounds good; the other is the real reason. With this in mind, it might be well for us all to see if we are giving God the place that He should have. Don't forget this truth: The biggest room in the world is the room for improvement. See you in church Sunday!

Attending Church Vital
To Sincere Churchgoer

Can we worship God as well at home as at church? If so, why go to church at all?

There are, perhaps, many reasons why different people go to church; the noblest reason is to worship God. Just because a few people go to church for ignoble purposes does not mean that worship is not vital to most churchgoers. There is more to vital worship than just merely bringing a carcass to a pew and parking it for a specific length of time. Real public worship is revitalizing.

Worship is spiritual communion with the Eternal. The fruit of this relationship is divine insight into the various problems of the individual soul. It is through worship that we find what God's will is for our lives. We come to the sanctuary and lay down our burdens and look at life from a vantage point at some infinite place in eternity. When we become in tune with the Father of the Universe, we can look at life with all its problems and temptations as He does. We can realize what is really important in the world. Today always looks different from Eternity.

The Sabbath is a gift from God; it meets a basic human need. This means that we have one day in a week that we can live more like we will live in Eternity. A part of the Sabbath is for public worship; but, all the day is to be used as sacred and holy. It was never meant for the Sabbath to be only sixty minutes in seven days. The Scripture reveals to us that this day should be used for worship, rest, and doing good. Participating in public worship reminds us of our sacred responsibilities and obligations as "sons of God." Our thoughts are centered on holy things. Those things that are ugly, vulgar, and mean are flushed from our thoughts. Through this power of God's grace, life becomes vital and challenging. If this does not happen to you, it is because you do not participate in spiritual worship. It is as important that you do your own worshipping as it is that you do your own eating or thinking, but in public worship, each is seeking to find God's will, making the atmosphere more conducive to spiritual perception.

Yes, you can worship God at home, or on a golf course, or somewhere else other than God's sanctuary on Sunday morning at the set time for worship, but if you are not there, except for providential reasons, it becomes rather obvious that you are not too serious about your religious responsibilities. If everyone should follow in your steps, the church bells would stop ringing, the pews would all be vacant, and the church doors would be closed! Don't hoodwink yourself with cheesecloth excuses. Wise up to the facts of life! Hope to see you in church Sunday!

Brotherhood's Concept
Is Key To World Peace

Brotherhood is a big word! If the peoples of the world had a proper concept of this word, wars would become obsolete and racial prejudice would become a thing of the past. There are some who divest this word of its proper meaning by limiting it to include only those of their own household, caste, or special group. There are others who look at the idea of brotherhood with a vision of the entire world. This latter concept is the urgent need for peace and security.

Modern science has moved the foreigner into our back yard. It is our responsibility to make him a friend instead of a foe. A century ago he was so far away that we could ignore him. It is not that way today. Modern transportation has made the most distant spot on the globe only a matter of a few hours away, and it is only a split second away by present day communication. If fact, a radio wave travels so fast that it could originate in Honolulu and travel around the world seven times and arrive in New York on the eighth loop in one second. This is quite a fabulous age in which we are living.

The time has come when we must think of the whole world as one neighborhood, or else...! We can work together and have a world of peace and happiness. Hate and discord can be replaced with love and good will. War and poverty can be substituted by peace and security. Prejudice and race superiority can be superseded by truth and mutual understanding. The key to this Utopia is the proper concept of brotherhood.

That sounds good doesn't it? But...? What can I do to make this dream a reality? You can do much! You can sweep out the attic of your mind and throw to the trash heap any prejudice and ill will toward any human being, or any thought about race superiority that may have accumulated through the years. You are your brother's keeper! You can accept that responsibility now and act accordingly.

Gift Of Love Praised By
Paul As Best Of All

The greatest thing in the world is love. To love and be loved makes life pleasant and enjoyable. Without love, the home would disintegrate, and the husband would go his way and the wife would go her way, leaving the children unwanted and unloved. Without love, the nation would fall, because no one would be interested in living by its laws or dying for its principles. Without love, the world would have no social order, because there would be no spiritual and moral gravity to hold it together.

The members of the early Corinthian church had many wonderful gifts from God. Some had great knowledge and wisdom; some had great faith and even the gifts of healing; and, others could work miracles and do mighty works in the name of Christ. However, there was one great hindrance to this church, and that was that they did not love one another as they should. So the Apostle Paul wrote them a letter and told them that the gift of love was worth more than all their other gifts put together. In fact, this gift of love is so far ahead of the other gifts that everything else, including tongues, knowledge, faith, and the sacrificing of one's body, is vain and absolutely worthless, without this gift of love.

To love God and to love our fellowman ought to be the ambition of all. If we do not have this gift, then it is our privilege and responsibility to seek it with our whole hearts, because it is the gift above all other gifts to be coveted. Love is connected with divine things, because God is love. We come to God through faith, but we become like him in love. If your Bible is handy, why not read what Paul said about this greatest thing in the entire world — Love. You can find this in I Corinthians 13:1-13.

Heavenly Rewards Come
From The Wise Use Of Time

You are familiar with the old adage: "Life is what you make it." Herein lies a truth that, perhaps, few of us have ever realized. It suggests that we are not to live our lives in a haphazard way; but, we are to make the most of life by planning our steps and directing our thoughts. We all have the same 24 hours a day in which to work. We begin in the cradle destitute of all material wealth. There are so many things in life common to all. Yet, some people live abundant lives, while others eke out only gloom and depression.

May we examine this 24-hour day to see if we are using it wisely? We usually think of it in terms of work, rest, and recreation. We all agree that it is our duty and privilege to accomplish eight honest working hours in a workday. For our health, it seems to be a consensus of opinion that we need about eight hours of sleep. We spend another hour eating, shaving, bathing, etc. So, it leaves us with a few extra hours to do as we please.

Someone has said about these off-duty hours: "There just ain't nothing to do!" In his despondency he folds his hands, drops his head, and refuses to live. Life becomes miserable, and so he looks for a scapegoat to blame for his condition. It may be the place of residence, temperature of the weather, his associates, his wife, his commander, or it may be that his parents gave him a bad start in life. In his search for a scapegoat, he forgets that life can be good, if only he will make it that way.

It matters little whether we live in an age of chivalry or in one of atom bombs, because we have about the same basic ingredients to build a life. Common sense teaches us that there is about as much to do now as there ever was. The place, weather conditions, or the possession of the "cattle upon a thousand hills" does not make the difference between happiness and despondency. The sportsman can pursue his interests; the scholar can advance his education; everyone can enjoy the luxury of friendship. There are hundreds of interesting hobbies for the person who is not "dead."

By the way, if time gets too heavy on your hands, why not go over to your church on Sunday and spend an hour or two in quiet meditation and worship of God, thanking Him for the blessings He has bestowed on you and your family. He appreciates an occasional sincere THANK YOU!

The Memory Bank

We may not have much money to put in the Bank of America, but we store memories in our personal Memory Bank every day to draw on in the future. Good memories will rise up to bless us. But the bad memories will jump on us to haunt us. So the wise person is concerned about storing up good memories to put in the Memory Bank each day.

I assume that it is true of all of us in that we have many memories. Some are good, and some are not so good. Oftentimes we would like to go back "and cross the bridge again," but of course, that is not possible. So the wise man stores up good memories to put in his Memory Bank. We need to discriminate with our thought patterns and bring up the thoughts that are worthy and wholesome. Even if our Memory Bank is low on funds, we can do like my folks used to tell me, "Do the best you can with what you have!"

Many things come along daily that trigger some of our memories. I remember that when I was a teenage we went to the Ringling Brothers and Barnum Bailey Circus in Wichita Falls, Texas. It was exciting to see the clowns, the animals, the animal trainers, and the trapeze actors. It was unbelievable to see the people jumping in midair to catch someone else in midair. It was breathtaking!

It was one of those red-letter days for me, but the greatest memory of eternal value happened on the way to the circus. On one of the street corners somewhere in Wichita Falls, Texas was a man singing the familiar song, "Down at the Cross." He sang with gusto,

> "Down at the Cross where my Savior died,
> Down where for cleansing from sin I cried,
> There to my heart was the blood applied;
> Glory to His name!...."

His poise and ability to sing and to give his testimony stood out more than all the performers of the circus. I never saw the man before or after, and I have no clue as to his background or his name. About all that I know about him was that he represented the Salvation Army. But he gave me an eternal blessing that day that was indelibly impressed on my mind. There were many people going in every direction that day, and whether others heard him or not I do not know. I just know that he set the chords of that song ringing in my ears that day, and I still hear him singing. Since that day, we have sung that song many times in the church. Every time I hear it, I am back again on that street corner somewhere in Wichita Falls, Texas listening to that man singing with such gusto, "Glory to His name."

So each day is precious! Where shall we go to give and receive precious memories for our Memory Bank? And how can we share our lives with someone? Maybe a smile or a kind word to a stranger would be an eternal blessing to that person. If we can fill our Memory Banks with good things, that will be of greater eternal value than all the Banks of America.

Only Through Prayer

After the Transfiguration Experience (Mark 9:2-13) Jesus, with Peter, James, and John, returned to the other disciples. There had been an argument raging between the disciples and the scribes. Jesus asked his disciples what they were arguing about. Verse 17 suggests that the argument was over the healing of a boy. They could not do it, so the priests were having a big time showing them up. The disciples had been with the Master for about 2 and half years, so they had seen healing on many occasions, but they failed to have the power to heal the boy. Jesus then healed the boy, and the people were amazed. Later, when they were in the house by themselves, the disciples asked Jesus, "Why were we not able to expel the demon?" Then Jesus said, "This kind cannot be driven out except by prayer." (Some manuscripts have "prayer and fasting," but the older manuscripts do not have "fasting.")

So "What is the power of prayer?" It is more than a formula of words to be repeated (Matthew 6:7). It is more than a repeat after me prayer. It is not telling God what needs to be done. And yet, I ask God for many favors!

When Jesus came, there was plenty of power to heal the boy. The father of the child begged Jesus to heal his son. He said, "...but if you can, have compassion on us and help us!" Then Jesus repeated his "if you can" statement and added, "All things are possible to him who believes."

We live in two worlds: the material and the spiritual. The Psalmist tells us that the angels of the Lord encamp about those who fear him. James tells us that Elijah was a man like us. He prayed, and it did not rain for three years and six months. Then he prayed and the rain came. Did that mean that Elijah had power to control the weather conditions? It is interesting to examine his prayer in 1 Kings 18:36, "O Lord, the God of Abraham, Isaac, and

Israel, let it be known this day that I am your servant and that I have done all these things at your word." So it was not Elijah's idea at all. He just found out what God was doing and fell in with him.

In 2 Kings 6: 8–23, the Syrian king was after Elisha and had surrounded him with horses and chariots. Elisha's servant was fearful. But Elisha said, "Fear not; for those with us are more than those with them." Then Elisha prayed a beautiful prayer, "Lord, I pray you, open his eyes that he may see." Then the servant saw the mountain full of horses and chariots of fire round about Elisha.

So then, what is the power of prayer? And why should we pray? It seems to be that we need to find out what God is doing and how we can work into his plans. And when we pray, it is not so much getting him to alter his plans, but it is how can we alter our plans to work into his program. It was God telling Elijah what he was up to and not Elijah thinking up a way to get the best of Ahab!

So Jesus said it was only through prayer that the demon could be cast out of the boy. So we need to find out what God is doing and become his voice for the consummation.

Communication

We are blessed with so many ways of communication in our times. We have telegraph, telephone, cell phones, fax machines, e-mail, radio, television, and electrical equipment that can cause you to reach for your ear plugs! Most of the modern communication systems have come into being since I arrived on the scene November 19, 1919.

The Winn Hill Community (midway between Fort Worth, Texas and Wichita Falls, Texas) was not connected very well with the world. We had heard about the telegraph, and we even had a telephone that was connected with Grandpa and Grandma, who lived a half mile west of us. At one time, I remember that we had strung up a line that went all the way to Uncle Jake and Aunt Amy. It was a rather sophisticated system with long and short rings to let people on the line know whom you were ringing. At one time there must have been six or eight people on the line. It worked when we had a good battery in the box and when the line was up all the way.

When I started to school, I walked with my older brother, Anthony. When we went over the hill and out of sight, there was no way to communicate with our parents until we came back in the afternoon. I remember that the mile and a half was a long walk. My mother was home all day long by herself. Pa worked on the farm and sometimes with his small herd of cattle. So when he left the house and was out of sight, there was no means of communication. If he worked near the house, he came in for dinner and about a fifteen-minute nap, and then he was back on the job.

Back in those days, we never missed the modern means of communication, because we never even dreamed that it could be a reality. However, there were a few "nuts" that brought up strange ideas sometimes in idle conversation. A few were saying that the time would come when people would be sending pictures through the air. But the idea was so farfetched and downright stupid that we did not give it a serious thought—about as impossible as a person going to the moon!

We did have a very efficient Postal System. So we could keep up with our friends and relatives who had moved away. We could send a letter anywhere in the USA for two cents and a post card for one cent. Virgil, Pa's brother, when he was about 20 years of age, got a job working with mules on a farm in Benjamin, Texas about  25 miles from home. One of the mules kicked him and he died. Before Grandma and Grandpa heard about it, Virgil had already been buried.

Isn't it great that today we are hooked up with the world? When something happens on the other side of the world, we hear about it in minutes. We have three telephones in our home—one is on my desk, and I have a cell phone— and we have several radios, televisions, and a computer that is hooked up with the world. Let us ever be aware of the awesomeness of modern communication and the responsibility that goes along with it. May we be good stewards of the blessings of communication, and let us always have a word of encouragement to those who will receive it!

The Honey Bee

The honeybee is a very important insect. We usually think of honeybees because of the honey produced by them, but their value as a pollinator is of greater importance. The great majority of the hundreds of species of bees in the world live solitary, unsocial lives like flies, grasshoppers, and most other insects, but the honeybee is a social insect. Prior to 1500 there were no honeybees in the New World. The early settlers took hives of bees with them to their new homes. There is no record of honeybees in North America until 1638.

I was first introduced to the honeybee when I was a young lad. Pa liked to hunt the bees and eat their honey, and he brought bee colonies home and put them in our peach orchard. One summer, I remember that he had about 13 colonies in our orchard. One time, he bought a queen bee from Sears, Roebuck & Company, and in the wintertime he put her and her brood in the loft of the barn with hay surrounding the hive. The bees did not survive the winter. Years later, I can see why they did not survive. We were disappointed, but the experience with the bees gave me a lifelong interest in beekeeping.

The honeybee is a social insect. The colony is made up of three social ranks: a queen, hundreds of male drones, and 20,000 to 80,000 workers. The queen and the drones are fertile, and their main functions are reproductive. The sterile female worker bees do all the work: they build the hives, ward off enemies, collect food, feed the queen and drones, and nurse the young.

The queen lays eggs in the cells, and she puts sperm in some of the cells. The unfertilized eggs develop into drones. Fertilized eggs develop into queens or worker bees — depending on the type of food given them by the worker bees. All the bees have a job to do. The worker bees fan out from the hive to find the needed nectar. When they have found it, they bring it back to the hive, and with a wagtail dance, they tell the other bees where it is so that they can also get the supply to bring it back to the hive. When the honey flow is over, they do not need the drones, because the hive will not be swarming and it must conserve the food supply to survive. Therefore, they liquidate the drones. When the queen gets too old to function properly, they supersede her, and the old workers that are too feeble to produce are also destroyed.

It takes the queen 16 days to hatch, the drones 24 days, and the worker bee 21 days. After hatching, the worker bee spends its first 21 days on house duty, and its last 21 days are spent on outside duties. So, for a hive to be healthy, there must be lots of bees hatching out to replace the older ones. However, in wintertime the worker bees live longer. So, when Pa robbed a hive and put the colony in a box in the peach orchard, the bees had to make new cells before the queen could lay eggs. By the time the cells were prepared, the older bees were dying off, and by the time the first batch of bees emerged from their cells there were not many bees left. When the hive was small, it gave the moths the opportunity to come in and devastated the hive.

We, here in Bryan, Texas, live only a few miles from the "bee capitol of the world." The Weavers at Lynn Grove have been in the beekeeping business for more than a century. They sell about 45,000 queens each year throughout the USA and to foreign countries. So if you ever want to learn more about beekeeping just visit their apiaries sometime.

My Church

Let me tell you about my church. I have been preaching since 1940. I have never had big crowds, but for  the most part I have had someone to preach to most every Sunday since that day in March when I preached my first sermon. My church is a small church, and we usually have about 40 people for the Morning Worship Service. We are not a wealthy church, nor are we a prestigious church, but our church has a compassion for all who come our way. A few Sundays ago, we had a very interesting group of people. We had people from Africa (our associate pastor and his wife and family are from Nigeria, Africa); there were several from Mexico (Lety Johnson, who plays the guitar and helps lead the music program is from Mexico); Stephanie Etchells, who sings with our singing group, was from Canada; and, Olga Marantidi, who plays the piano for our offertory, was from Russia. Nai Meng Phillips, who is from Laos and was with us for several years, sends us her heartfelt greetings from California, where she now resides. And Chuck Blend, who is a Christian Jew, has been worshipping with us for several Sundays.

The amazing thing is that this has come about without publicity, and those who have come from varied cultures have blended together to become an integral part of the family of God. Our ministry is unique. We have our regular Sunday worship services and Wednesday evening Bible studies and Prayer meetings. We have a children's program that reaches out to the community, and we have had the privilege of ministering to many who have had no contact with the church. We have a Shelter to minister to homeless women and children who have no place to go. We have a garden ministry to serve the shelter and the community at large, and  we have a language ministry to teach Greek and Hebrew to anyone who is interested in reading the Bible in its original language. That is my church, and I like it. We seek to be a servant church, because Jesus said that was the way to true greatness. I used to think about the ideal church as a haven of shelter for all who come by. And least of all, I never realized that one day I would be a part of that fellowship.

Stewart Albert Newman

When I was a young man, Stewart Albert Newman was my pastor. We both grew up on farms. The Newman farm was about 4 or 5 miles southwest of our farm. After Dr. Newman graduated from college and the seminary, he became the Registrar and a professor at Southwestern Baptist Theological Seminary, Seminary Hill, near Fort Worth, Texas. He was called to be pastor of his childhood church, the First Baptist Church of Jermyn, Texas. The distance from the seminary to Jermyn was about 70 miles. His parents still lived on the old home place. So. that would be his weekend headquarters for the next several years as he pastored the Jermyn church.

I grew up in the Winn Hill community. We were about 4 miles east of Jermyn. My church was Bethany Baptist Church in the Winn Hill community. Our church also called Dr. Newman to be our pastor. He accepted the call. So he would preach at Jermyn in the morning services and come to our church twice each month for an afternoon service. As pastor, he also arranged for revival meetings in the summertime. So, it was in those days that I was privileged to sit at the feet of one of the greatest preachers that I have ever known. He was a great scholar, and yet he was at home with the common man. It was through him that I learned that dedicated scholarship was not opposed to, but a part of, Christian holiness. It was a surprise to learn that the King James Authorized Version is only one of other translations of the Word of God.

During this time, the Lord called me to preach the Good News. So it was Dr. Newman who gave me leadership at this time of my preparation for the Gospel ministry. I wanted to immediately enter the seminary. But Dr. Newman told me that I must finish my college degree before I entered the seminary. I took his advice, because I realized that he was right. He gave me opportunities to preach. So through his encouragement, I preached my first sermon in March 1940. At that time I was 20 years of age.

For over a year, beginning in the summer of 1940, I left school where I had been attending, NTSTC, and came back to the farm. I became obsessed in my reading and studying the Bible. During that time I had opportunities to preach, and sometimes Dr. Newman would invite me to preach at the Bethany Baptist Church. I shall never forget the subtle ways of his teaching. One of his great lessons he taught me after one of my sermons. I had been listening to a radio preacher by the name of E. F. Webber, who boasted of the fact that he would be on the air until Jesus comes back in the air. He had a book to prove it. I got his book, and I was pretty well convinced that Jesus was coming very soon. So I thought I should preach a sermon on that same subject. I think that Dr. Newman was disappointed with my prophetic message. He did not say much, but after the service was over, he took me behind some of the cars in the parking lot. I cannot remember all he said — actually only a few words — but I do remember the gist of the conversation. It went something like this: "It has been many years since Jesus was here, and it may be a few more years before he gets back." He was calm and kind and I did not feel scolded, but I can assure you that I have never preached that sermon again!

That first year of my ministry was on the farm working with my parents (Ma & Pa). As I look back I can see it was a wonderful year for me. My library was a King James Bible, and I studied and marked each page from Genesis to Revelation. So my library consisted of one book, but during that time my library was doubled! It was a thrill to get a book from Dr. Newman. It was wrapped in brown paper and addressed to: Rev. Clyde Wilton. Yes, it actually was to "Rev. Clyde Wilton." It was the first time I had ever seen my name connected to "Rev." And on the inside it said: "To Clyde

Wilton with the best regards of Stewart A Newman, July 21, 1940. It was "How to Prepare Sermons and Gospel Addresses," by William Evans. I have taken that book with me ever since that day. That book is not for sale. Just to see it brings back many precious memories of the man who always gave me good advice.

Later, when I was in the seminary, Dr. Newman let me use a little plot of his land for a garden. I was excited to use it. I cultivated and planted some seed, but, as well as I can remember, the weeds took over. So I did not do much with it. He was probably disappointed with me again, but he never told me so. He always gave me encouragement. Over the years we have corresponded by letter. I was delighted to see and hear the video of his 90th birthday. When he passed away, I was saddened, but I have those precious memories in our memory bank that shall always be with me. Praise the Lord for the life of Stewart A. Newman!

Complaining

Life is precious to some people, but it is a drag to others. The disposition of the individual makes the difference. Henry Ward Beecher said, "Good nature, like a bee, collects honey from every herb. Ill nature, like the spider, sucks poison from the sweetest flower." Cicero said, "A perverse and fretful disposition makes any state of life unhappy." And, J. F. Clarke said, "The root of all discontent is self-love."

So how shall we use the day that the Lord has given us? We may choose to complain and grumble about things we do not like, or we can rejoice in the wonderful blessings that the Lord has given us. I was reminded of this when we went to Hawaii for a tour of duty in the Air Force, from 1952 to 1955.

It was a cold, miserable winter at Chanute Air Force Base in Rantoul, Illinois when we were reassigned to Hickam Air Base in Oahu, Hawaii. When we arrived in Hawaii, the beauty of the place was everywhere we looked. The temperature was ideal the entire year—never very hot, or never very cold. I remember talking to a lady who was complaining about, of all things, the weather! In Hawaii, there were never the traditional seasons, and she did not like that at all. There were never the blue northers from the North Pole or blistering heat from the Equator—just the same pleasant weather all the time. So it became monotonous with her.

There was another time that I had an interesting conversation with an officer in the city of Wahiawa, Oahu. I do not remember much about him, but I remember that he was an officer with the rank of major and that he had children in school there. His complaint was about the schools in Hawaii. Personally, I had not detected any inferiority in the school system, but for the sake of the conversation I admitted that might be possible. However, I suggested that the variety of people from so many cultures made it possible for our children to receive a course in Race Relations. That thought ticked him off, and he said, "I am from Texas and I am not interested in my children having that course!" I retorted by saying, "I am also from Texas and I am pleased for my children to have that course." That ended our conversation, but the friendly encounter became an eternal part of my memory.

Then there were those airmen from New York that were disgusted with their assignment in Hawaii. There complaint was, "There is nothing to do here!" So it is that we can all be in the same place, and some can find things to complain about and others can find things to rejoice about, and each of us must make the choice. Time it precious for those who know how to use it, and in using it wisely we will not waste our time complaining.

Who Is The Greatest?

Jesus and Peter, James, and John came down from the glorious time of the Transfiguration experience and returned to the other apostles, and from there they all went to Capernaum. When they arrived in Capernaum and went into the house, Jesus asked them what they had been arguing about on the way. The word διελογίζεσθε means to discuss, to dispute. The context suggests that they had been arguing. Jesus was trying to teach the apostles about the cross. They must have been ashamed of themselves for they were silent, because they had been arguing with one another about who is the greatest. They were still thinking that Jesus was going to set up a political kingdom, and they were thinking that they ought to have top jobs. That does bring up a very important question: who is the greatest?

How do we arrive at greatness? Is it a matter of prestige, wealth, education, status, or personal wit? I suppose that every one of us has the desire to become great—perhaps more in the eyes of people than in the eyes of God. So we like to compare ourselves with others who have achieved less than ourselves.

Who are the great people? Some would say that Osama bin Laden is a great person, and others would put Ted Turner or Bill Gates on the top shelf. And how shall we evaluate men like Michael Jordan and Mohammed Ali?

What part does Sacrifice have in relation to Greatness? Jesus put great importance on the Cross. In fact, it is central in the teaching of the Gospel. Jesus said that if we are not willing to take up our cross, then we cannot be his disciples. And yet Paul said that if we "give our bodies to boast" we are profited nothing if we do not have love. We think of the suicide bombers in Palestine today and see that they are ready to make sacrifices, but are they great? Sacrifice has a place, but is that enough for real greatness?

Then there is Ambition, and how does it work in with Greatness. Alexander conquered so many nations that they called him "Alexander the Great!" Napoleon, Hitler, and Stalin were ambitious, and they had millions to follow them, but did they achieve greatness? Ted Turner and Bill Gates are ambitious and have the wealth of this world, but have they achieved greatness?

Jesus summed it up in a very interesting way. He said that greatness has to do with service. "If anyone wants to be first, he must be last and servant of all." So I guess that about sums it up. That puts greatness in the reach of us all, if we are willing to pay the price.

So greatness has to do with attitude. The glory seeker may be trying to compete with the greatest, to be better with no concern for his/her welfare. The other extreme is the person who seeks out the needy to make life more blessed for the recipient. To the one, greatness is to seek the glory of the world, and to the other, greatness is in the glory of Christ. Are we still interested in being one of the greatest! Only God will keep the score.

According to Thomas A. Kempis, "Thou art not the better because thou art praised, nor the worse because thou art dispraised. For as thou art thou art, and whatsoever may be said of thee, thou art no better than Almighty God, who looketh upon the heart will witness thee to be!"

It Is Time To Forgive

It is a wonderful privilege to have the ability to forgive. If we do not forgive others their sins against us, we cannot receive forgiveness of our sins against God (Matthew 6: 14-15). We are desperately in need of God's forgiveness; otherwise, we can never enjoy the sweet fellowship of walking with the Almighty. To live with wrath, anger, grudges, hostility, and hatred leads to bitterness and failure. Our God is the epitome of goodness, mercy, and love. When we receive his forgiveness, we receive his attributes.

It is not uncommon for church people to live with hostility and grudges. I remember when I was a teenager, that happened in our family. We lived on a small farm of 132 ½ acres in North Texas. We also leased a 14-acre piece of land about a mile from our house. For several years, we used the land for cotton and other farm products. Mr. Edmondson, the owner of the land, lived 275 miles away in Wheeler, Texas. In those days, travel was slow, and we seldom ever saw him. After several years of our tilling the soil on the Edmondson Place, the owner sold the land. He did not sell it to us, but he sold it to a neighbor who lived on a farm adjoining the land. My mother was devastated! She thought that because we had farmed that land for so many years, we ought to have had first opportunity to buy it. She became so angry that her hostility extended not only to the neighbor's immediate family but also to all his relatives. This grudge lasted for years.

A strange and wonderful thing happened to change her hate into love. When I was in college, the Lord called me to preach the Gospel. It was my privilege to go back to my little home church in the country and preach my first sermon. Dr. S. A. Newman was the pastor, and after I had preached the sermon, Dr. Newman took a collection for me. The regular membership was about 20 members, but that day the one room building was filled. They passed the plate and in that plate was a check for $5.00. Now $5.00 was something in those days, because in those days a postage stamp was 3 cents, a hamburger was 5 cents, and you could get a shave and a haircut for two bits (25 cents). Money was very scarce with us, so that was a large gift. The signature of the check was Jim Crum, and he was the man who bought the Edmondson Place.

Not long after that, I overheard my mother telling someone about the check, and she said that the ill will was gone. One act of kindness had removed years of hostility. The Good Book tells us that vengeance belongs to God. So we should let God take care of any wrongs or imaginary wrongs done against us. To live in the sunshine of God's grace means that we must forgive others. Then God can forgive us, and that will take away all grudges and hostility against others. What time is it? It is time to forgive!

Casual Learning

We think that schools are very important, and we go to school for many years to get an education. We want our children to get ahead, so we try to provide for them the best of opportunities for learning. So it is obvious that formal learning is important, but we should never forget that casual learning is often times more impressive. Some of our most impressive lessons in life are learned by experience rather than by lecture.

When I was a young boy playing in from of our house by the roadside, I received a lesson in nature that I shall never forget. I was playing in the dirt and I saw one of the most colorful bugs that I had ever seen. So I picked it up, but only for a moment! Wow! What a sting that bug had! It sent me to the house crying. No one needed to lecture me about picking up bugs any more! The parents may be careful to teach their children to keep their hands off the stove, but that may not be as impressive as an experience of getting their hands burned. All through life we have experiences that modify our behavior. Ben Franklin was right when he said, "Experience keeps a dear school, yet Fools will learn in no other." (Poor Richard's Almanac, 1743).

I shall never forget a lesson I had in English Grammar. It was casual learning, but it was so impressive that it changed my speech pattern. I was a sophomore (the word is made up with two Greek words that mean "wise moron" or "wise fool") in college. So I was in college and knew most everything that made one wise. I was hitchhiking to go home for a few days, and a lady in a car picked me up and gave me a ride from Denton to Fort Worth, Texas. I was busy telling the lady about "what I seen." Then she proceeded to tell me that since I was in college, I ought to know that to use seen it must always have a helper (have, has, or had) to go along with it. She took all the air out of my balloon, and I have forgotten what I was telling her. However, I have since never forgotten to use "seen" only with a helper. That was learning by intimidation. So all through life we learn by the experiences we have. The classroom lectures are important, but no more important that casual learning.

Grandpa Rhoades

I would like to tell you about my mother's father, Grandpa Rhoades. He was an old-timer who was born on the other side of the Mississippi River. He settled in Jack County long enough for his daughter, Eula May, my mother, to grow up and get married to my Pa, Elmer Wilton. Then Grandpa moved west and finally ended up in Childress, Texas. Some of his children went on west as far as California. So when I was a boy we went to Childress, Texas about every two years visiting Grandpa and Grandma Rhoades. I was not around him very much, but there were a few things that I vividly remember about him. He was uneducated, very strong, and I was told that he was a good checker player. His son, my Uncle Bob, was also a great checker player. Maybe that's how I acquired a great love for the game of checkers.

I remember one time Grandpa visited us when I was a boy, and he told me a story about his teeth that I shall never forget. At that time he was an old man, and he had all his own teeth—firm and solid—except for one that had been crushed and had sharp points on it. That tooth had given him terrible pain, so he took a pair of pliers and crushed it. The pain finally left him, but the crushed tooth remained with him for the rest of his life. His teeth were discolored from smoking a pipe, but they were solid. And he told me why he had such a solid mouthful of teeth. According to him, he had never messed up his teeth with a toothbrush, "because brushing your teeth brushes the enamel away and destroys your teeth." So that was his reason for his solid set of teeth.

Grandpa's language was from the past, but that's how he learned it. For instance, he "seed" certain things. He used "seed" for the past tense of "to see." As I think about it, "seed" would be the logical past tense of "to see." However, English is not always logical. Somewhere along the way, "saw" got in the picture and outlawed "seed" from the

165

common language of the people. But I guess he never knew about the change, since did not bother with reading books.

I think that he was about 70 years of age when he passed away. I was told that after retirement he occasionally went back to his workplace and played checkers with his gang. On one occasion, two men were trying to lift a heavy plank to move it, and they could not. So Grandpa went over, picked it up by himself, and moved it where they wanted to take it. He was a strong man; however, that lift caused him to have internal bleeding. That night he went home and died. He was an interesting man, my Grandpa Rhoades. I didn't know him very well because we lived so far away and could not visit very often. I wish I could have known him better.

The Need For Friends

The need for friends is great. We need to have friends so we can share our lives with them. Without friendship, life becomes dull and meaningless. We can be in a large city with the mass of people going in all directions and yet be lonely it there is no one to enjoy a close fellowship with.

Yes, we need friends. Early in life we sense a great need for people who care for us and are compatible for developing a friendship with us. This friendship usually develops first in the family unit. We have memories of those days when we were babies, and the tender care of our parents go with us throughout life.

I vividly remember my early days on a small farm in North Texas. My parents were poor, in reference to material things, but I never doubted their love for me. We would go to Jacksboro (a big city of about 4,000 people) about twice a month to shop for groceries. I fondly remember that Pa would buy me a nickel's worth of candy in a small paper sack, and sometimes he would get me a plug of chewing gum.

Then, one day I went off to college. I left my mother in tears, because she did not want to see her baby boy leave home.

College life was new to me. I had to provide for myself. My lifestyle was drastically changed. I met new friends, and that was a wonderful experience for me. I thought I could handle anything that came my way. One new rude awakening was when I tried to iron my white shirt. After I burned a hole in the sleeve, I decided it would be cheaper for me to send my shirts to the laundry. I roomed with some other young college students, and we all needed to have something to eat. So I thought I could cook pinto beans. With five hungry boys, we needed plenty to eat, so I got the big dishpan and filled it full of pinto beans and turned up the heat. Sometime later, the aroma of burned beans filled the house. I was beginning to appreciate what my parents had done for me over the years. The stench of those burned beans still lingers in my nostrils!

It was a thrill to be away from home and to live with other young men of my age. But I remember my longing to go back home and be with my parents and friends once more. Finally the day came. Pa met me in Jacksboro one Saturday afternoon. When I was a kid I thought about what he could give me, such as candy and chewing gum. But now the thrill was not what he could give me, but the thrill was just to be in his presence again and to talk to him and enjoy his friendship.

What about our friendship with our heavenly Father? When we are babes in Christ, we are concerned about what he can do for us. We ask for many things, and indeed, we need his provisions for our survival. But when we grow up spiritually, we become more concerned about his daily presence. We come to realize that the most awesome experience in the entire world is to have sweet fellowship with the Almighty God who created us. He is a friend of all friends, and his friendship gives meaning to life. And with him, we can soar above the circumstances of life and rejoice and be glad in each day he gives us. Praise the Lord for his friendship!

Is Your Church A Building?

The Greek word κυριακός is an interesting word. It is an adjective derived from the noun κύριος (Lord) in the sense of "owner" and meaning "of the lord or owner." The word is used twice in the New Testament. In 1 Corinthians 11:20 it is the Lord's Supper, and in Revelation 1:10 it is the Lord's Day. It is from that word that we get our word for church, and it means the Lord's House. The  word "church" is an Anglo Saxon word, "circe," and from Greek κυριακός the Lord's House. The dictionary definition of the word is,

"1. A building for public religious worship.
2. A religious service held in such a building.
3. An organized body of Christians."

What is your concept of the church? What would you say if someone should ask you, "Where is your church?" Would you say, "It is on the corner of 24th and Houston streets," or some other geographical location? It is common to equate the church with a building. We take pride in our beautiful and luxurious buildings. We must have central heat in the wintertime and air conditioning in the summertime.  The stained glass windows set the atmosphere for worship. The soft cushions on the pews let us worship in comfort, and the electronic equipment gives us quality in worship. The building can be the pride of the religious community. The building may be the largest and most beautiful in the city, but is that your church?

When Jesus established the church, there were no buildings involved. When Peter made his profession of faith, Jesus said that he would build his church on that confession of faith. So Jesus built his church on spiritual reality rather than on buildings. The church was not concerned about buildings until many years later. So where is the discrepancy? The fact is that the word Jesus used for church was ἐκκλησία which means "a called out people." Jesus and the church of the New Testament days were not interested in buildings. They  were interested in sharing the gospel of salvation to a lost world. They shared the good news on the streets, in the homes of the believers, and down by the riverside—just any place they could find people who would listen to them.

Where is the church? The church that Jesus established is not a building. It is where the people are. The building is secondary and should never be the driving force of the congregation. Praise God for our buildings, but let us always remember that our calling is missions and evangelism and not just comfortable buildings to retreat from rough edges of the world.

From A Worm To A Butterfly

I have been working on Mark 9. I finished the spreadsheet of 860 words — it took about 3 days to do it. So, now I have finished the translation of the chapter, and I have prepared notes for a sermon on the subject of The Transfiguration of Jesus. An important Greek word in this connection is μετεμορφώθη. Our English word metamorphosis comes from that word, and it means transformation — a change of form. It is used 4 times in the New Testament. One of these is in 2 Corinthians 3:18, where, as believers, we partake in the glory of Christ and are being changed into his likeness. As we gaze at him as in a mirror we are changed from glory to glory – that is, we become more like him. The reference here is to the process of Christian sanctification.

In Romans 12:2, there is another usage where we have the opportunity of being transformed into the likeness of Christ. We are not to be συσχηματίζεσθε conformed to this age, but we are to be μεταμορφαῦσθέ transformed by the renewing of the mind, that we may prove (or find out) what the will of God is.

The other two places are Matt. 17:2 and Mark 9:2 which is about the transfiguration of Jesus. In Luke, we are also told about the experience of the transfiguration, but he used other words to describe it.

The idea that comes to mind is the picture of the beautiful butterfly that is transformed (and that is the word used to describe the change from a worm to a butterfly — metamorphosis) from a worm that has no beauty to a butterfly with many beautiful colors.

So what is the conclusion of the whole matter? Are we going to be stuck in the embryo as a worm and never go through the stages of metamorphosis? If we use our time wrapped up in self and living in the negative — hanging on to grudges, hostilities, self pity, etc. — we will never make it to the beautiful stage of the butterfly!

The Voice Of God

The Holy Bible tells us about the Eternal Creator talking to his Creation on many occasions. The dialogue first began in the Garden of Eden when Adam and Eve "heard the voice of the Lord God walking in the garden in the cool of the day." They hid themselves and the Lord God called out to Adam, "Where are you?" Is the Lord God still trying to get the attention of his creation?

When Samuel was a young lad, he lived in the temple with Eli, the priest. One evening Samuel heard the voice of the Lord, but he thought it was Eli. After this happened three times, Eli realized that the Lord was speaking to Samuel, so he told him to go back to his bed and to answer the Lord when he spoke. Then it happened. Samuel talked with the Lord, and the Lord told Samuel what was going to happen. This was the beginning of the wonderful ministry of Samuel.

There are many such experiences of how the Lord communicated with his people. One very vivid encounter is the time he spoke to Elijah. After Elijah had been greatly used by the Lord, he became discouraged and so despondent even to the point of wanting to die. Then Elijah, fearful of Jezebel, fled to Horeb and spent the night in a cave. While he was there, he witnessed a might storm, an earthquake, and a fire. He was waiting for a word from the Lord. The hurricane, the earthquake, and the lightening were mighty demonstrations of the majesty of God, but he did not hear the voice of God through them. God disclosed himself to Elijah in the peaceful calm after the tempest. There are different translations of 1 Kings 19:12. KJV has it as "a still small voice," Goodspeed has "the sound of a gentle whisper," the New English Bible has "a low murmuring sound," the Jerusalem Bible has "the sound if a gentle breeze," but I am inclined to agree with Carlyle Marney's translation of "dead silence." The word is used only three times (1 Kings 19:12; Job 4:16; Ps. 107:29) and the literal meaning is silence. This is one of the ways that God still speaks to his people.

Does God still communicate with his creation? I was pastor of a small country church in 1943 in the Winn Hill Community, a few miles west of Jacksboro, Texas. We were meeting each day under the tabernacle for the summer Revival Meeting of the church. I used a familiar Psalm for my sermon subject one morning, and after the service Grandma Crum (Mrs. H. A. Crum) came to me and said, "We must be hooked up together because I read that scripture before I left the house this morning." That was rather strange, but it happened again that same week a few days later. But the second time it was in an obscure place. As well as I can remember, it was somewhere in the book of Kings. But her testimony was again that she read that same Scripture before she left the house. That has been 60 years ago, but I often remember what Mrs. Crum said and believe that the Lord was preparing her for the meeting. Yes, God does work in mysterious ways, his wonders to perform. God spoke to Samuel that night in bed in the temple; he communicated to Elijah at the entrance of a cave on Mt. Horeb one day; he prepared Mrs. Crum for the revival meeting that summer day at Winn Hill; and, I believe that he still communicates with his people today.

Jermyn High School

I grew up in the Winn Hill Community. So that is where I first went to school. All of our classes were in the same room, and we had one teacher, who was one of my best. Our teacher was "Miss Edna." Actually, her other name was Meyers, which was later changed to Shields, but for me it was "Miss Edna." She gave us little New Testaments and that was a gift that I will never forget. When I was in the 2nd or 3rd grade, our school consolidated with Jermyn. Later, during the 7th grade, that meant that we would ride a school bus to Jermyn to go to school. I had been walking a mile and a half  to school at Winn Hill, but the school was 3 miles and a half to Jermyn, where my brothers at one time walked to school. So now, we would have a bus to take us to school. How exciting it was! I remember that Sam Easter drove the bus part of the time. On rainy days, we had problems on a road by the Loving ranch that was called "the Long Lane," because in those days that road would get very muddy. It was always exciting to us when we got stuck in the mud and were late to class. Some days we were asked to get out and push, but as well as I can remember we were more interested in pushing the bus in a ditch than to get it back on the road tracks.

Jermyn was a great school. It was there where I met some lifelong friends. They were people who you never forget, like Eschol (Kink) Pruitt, Jamie McFadyen, Dale Hasson, Margaret Gillespie, Estelene Durham, and Mable Cope (those students were the members of our 1938 Graduation Class). We had teachers like Mr. Pryuer, W. F.

Cannon, Miss Prichard, and J. T. Jones (we often called him "Clabber mouth Jones" for some reason).

Back in those days, I had not been very far from Jermyn, Texas. So, when we went to Basketball Tournaments, those were great days for me! I usually spent the night with my friend Jamie McFadyen when we went off to the big games. I liked basketball very much, even though I was usually on the bench. I remember that we went to one of those big games at Post Oak (I believe that was the place). We played a team called Slidel (I had never heard about them before, nor have I since), but that team will never be forgotten! They would shoot the  ball from the middle (or before they got to the middle) of the court, and it would go through the basket. And as well as I can remember, it did not even hit the rim of the basket! That seemed to be taking the advantage of us, because we never even tried to shoot the ball that far back! But the umpire let them get by with it. I do not remember what the final score was, because it was one of those games you would rather not remember. They went on to win by running over the other teams as they did ours. So that made us feel a little better. They went home with the trophy, and we went home with new experiences!

My days at Jermyn High School are very vivid. That is when we got the new Brick School Building, and it was a beauty. The old one was a tall two-story, red brick building with big upstairs in the middle of the building. The new one was much better. We played ball in the playground just east of the building. There was a tennis court west of the building, a basketball gym northwest of the building, some bars that we played on just north of the building, and nearby there was the science building.

I always liked going to school (it was much better than working in the cotton patch or hoeing weeds in the garden), but I really was not interested in making good grades. In those days I thought I was doing fine if I operated at "C" level. I remember my cousins Herbert and Hazel Parrish would always make "A's," but I never understood the real difference until later. I realized that when I took a class of Mathematics under Herb (who was only about a month older than I) as one of the Math teachers of NTSTC. Yes, later I did learn that grades were important and that the opportunity to learn is precious. I later graduated from Howard Payne University and Southwestern Baptist Theological Seminary.

The Lord has been good to me. I met my wife, LaRue Vivian Haley, at Howard Payne College, and we were married at the Bethany Baptist Church at Winn Hill, Oct 1943. Our first son, Aaron, was born 1945 in Jacksboro, Texas; Fawncyne was next, and she was born 1950 in Bowie, Texas; Kathy was born 1953 in Tripler Army Hospital in Hawaii (we were  serving in the Air Force with duty at Wheeler Air Base, Hawaii); and, Stanley was born 1958 in Mission, Texas. I preached my first sermon in the Bethany Baptist Church in 1940, and I have been preaching ever since. Dr. S. A. Newman was our pastor. He was also pastor of the Jermyn Baptist Church. And he has always been my hero and ideal. He helped me get started, and he has always been a source of strength to me. I have been around the world but I always remember those days at Jermyn, Texas. Wherever I went I could never be far from Jermyn, Texas and the fond memories that I shall always cherish of those days. Those were indeed some of "the good old days" that we will never forget.

The Trip To Alaska

Life has a way of coming up with many opportunities and surprises. Some are good, and maybe some are not so good. I have wanted to see Alaska for many years, but I assumed that I would never have the opportunity to do so. But it happened!

Robert Worley, my son in-law, invited me to go along with him and Fawncyne, my daughter, for a vacation in Alaska. Robert has two sisters and two brothers-in-law in  Alaska. Robert and Fawncyne would be their guests while in Alaska, but how would I fit in, because they had not invited me? Robert assured me that they would accept me just like one of the family. So with that assurance, I said yes before they had time to back out. So, before the sun set that day I had purchased a ticket to Ketchikan, Alaska.

The vacation consisted of plans of fishing in the ocean and in the rivers. I was really not interested in fishing. My experience in deep-sea fishing was no more than a splitting headache. Years ago, I went deep-sea fishing off the coast of Honolulu, Hawaii and later off the coast of Port Isabel, Texas in the Gulf of Mexico. Both ended with miserable headaches. So I resolved never to go again. But this trip was different. Even though I was not interested in fishing, I was interested in seeing Alaska and being with Robert and Fawncyne and meeting new friends. So with glee I anticipated the trip to Alaska.

Bob and Terry Sivertsen live in Ketchikan, Alaska, and they were waiting for us when we arrived there at the Ketchikan International Airport, August 6, 2004. We had traveled all day, so it was nighttime when we arrived at the airport. The airport was across the bay from the city, so we had to catch a ferry to get to their house. My new friends were very gracious, and it was like Robert had told me. They immediately took me in like a member of their household. I was at home in the atmosphere of friendship and acceptance. And I had good food to eat and a comfortable bed to sleep in.

Ketchikan, with about 14,000 people, is the fourth largest city in Alaska. It is perched on the rocky southwestern shore of Revillagigedo Island, and it is a city isolated with no bridges to other islands or to the mainland. Ketchikan is a very important port, because almost half a million summer visitors make Ketchikan their first port of call. On the following day, Bob took us to Thorne Bay and to the City of Thorne Bay, and that was a day to remember.

We traveled in Bob's fishing boat. He has a wonderful boat with all the fishing gear needed for pulling in the salmon. His boat (valued at about 36,000 dollars) has a depth finder and an instrument that can put the fish bait at the designated depth, along with expensive assortments of rods and reels and nets to lift the fish to the boat. Bob is an interesting man. His father was a Norwegian and his mother was a native Alaskan of the Aleut peoples. He was born in Alaska and has lived in Alaska all his life, so he has the answers, if you have the questions about Alaska. Bob is employed by the city of Ketchikan, but he loves to catch fish. He likes the catching more than the fishing. The regular cost for four people using a boat of this caliber for four hours of fishing is $1,000.00, but for us it was free of charge! Wow! What a deal.

We traveled on the Alaskan International Highway from Ketchikan to Thorne Bay. On the way, Bob stopped by the side of the highway and gave us special instructions, and we threw out the lines. The salmon fish were going to the rivers to spawn. Two years before, they had hatched in the fresh water rivers; then they had gone to the big ocean to live most of their lives; and, now it was time for them to go home and spawn. They occasionally jumped out of the water, and in the rivers they were so thick that we could see them in bunches going upstream. So Bob knew where they were and how deep to put the baited hook. So he gave us the lines and we began bringing them in. As Bob had told us, catching is more fun than just fishing. So this trip was fun without the

headache! Before we arrived in the city of Thorne Bay, we had a tub full of beautiful salmon fish.

This was the beginning of a great week of catching, rather than just fishing. It was a time to remember. So I had to change my negative feelings about deep-sea fishing. Thanks to Bob Sivertsen, we learned many things about Alaska and enjoyed the fun of catching fish. He also worked on another project during our week with him. He spent several hours working with pictures that he took during the activities of the week, and when it was completed, he gave us CDs of pictures of some of the beautiful secrets of Thorne Bay.

So now we not only have memories of the week, but we have pictures to view again the beautiful scenes of the week, especially the gorgeous sunsets of Thorne Bay from the balcony of Nick and Wendy's mansion by the seashore. Bob was our hero, and when we think about Alaska, we will think about Bob and Terry Sivertsen, and Nick and Wendy Gefre, who gave us a week of sweet memories.

A Week In Thorne Bay, Alaska

Thorne Bay is about 45 miles from Ketchikan, but you can only go by air or water, because there are no roads for cars. So the only way to get there is by seaplane, ferry boat, or fishing boat. Bob Sivertsen took Robert, Fawncyne, and me by fishing boat from Ketchikan to Thorne Bay. There we stayed with Nick and Wendy Gefre and their beautiful daughters. Wendy was Robert's sister and Nick his brother in-law, and they accepted me as a new member of their household. Their beautiful house was at the edge of the seashore. The water at the edge of their yard rose and fell as

the tide came in and went out. The sunsets were the most beautiful I had ever seen. At the time of the sunset each day, we would go the balcony and take pictures of the gorgeous colors of the sunset.

Thorne Bay is on the Prince of Wales Island, which is the third largest island in the United States. Kodiak is first and the island of Hawaii is second. The City of Thorne Bay, with a population of 550, had been a logging city; therefore, many trees have been cut down, but new tees are taking their place. Nick is the owner of Petra Alaska, which supplies petroleum to the general area. Nick has a seaplane, so he daily checks his crab basket traps. One day he took me for a ride, and we flew over the bay and the mountains. We landed in the bay, and he gathered many large crabs form his baskets. In the evening we had plenty of crab to eat. The view from the air was spectacular. There were some houses floating in the bay. The landscape was filled with beautiful tall tees; however, the loggers had left some bald spots.

We also fished in the river that came into Thorne Bay. The fish were so thick we could see them swimming upstream. In one place Robert snagged one as they pulled his hook through the water. But it is not legal to catch them by snagging, so he had to throw it back in the water. They were going back to their birthplace to spawn. They had been in the ocean of salt water for two years, but now they were going back to the fresh water to spawn.

It is one of the secrets of God's creation that the salmon fish returns to spawn at the place of their birth and first two weeks of their lives. There are different species of salmon, and the King Salmon have five-year cycles; however, the salmon fist that we were catching had a two-year cycle. We are told that the female salmon makes a hole in the waterbed and deposits her eggs. The male salmon deposits sperm on the eggs. After the salmon fish spawn, they die. The eggs are hatched in the fresh water, but the adult salmon fish live their lives in the salt-water ocean somewhere, but no one knows just were it is. When the time comes to spawn they know how to get back to their original fresh water home. So we intercepted them on their way home.

We were there on Sunday, so Wendy took us to her church, which was affiliated with the Christian Missionary Alliance. It was a nice, friendly church, and I wanted to go to their mid-week Bible study, which was Thursday evening. The Bible study was across the bay at Wally Greentree's home, a member of the church. So he came in a skiff and took me across the bay to his home in the rain forest. He had worked for the forest service for many years. I was amazed at the size of the trees. Some of the cedars must have been 7 or 8 feet in diameter and 2 or 3 hundred feet tall. This was in a protected area, so they had never been cut down and they had about 150 inches of rain each year. The men were godly men, and the Bible study was inspirational.

Nick and Wendy were big-hearted hosts. The rooms were filled with guests, but they were gracious to have a place for us all. The house was filled with guests for one whole week, about 15 in number. Robert's sister, Mrs. Elaine Ritchie, and a close friend of the family, Ms. Thresh Hockett,  were there. They seemed to operate on the old principle that "there is room for one more." They gave me a comfortable place to sleep in the living room. So we will forever remember this week with special fondness. Thank-you, Nick and Wendy, for giving us a place to enjoy Alaska for a whole week.

Guyana, South America

Guyana is an interesting place. The Dutch were the first settlers to come to Guyana. They came there in the eighteenth century. The Dutch founded Demerara about 1745, where Georgetown is now, with plantations at the river

mouth. Much of the Northern part of Guyana is about 6 feet below sea level. So the Dutch built a sea wall for many miles to keep the Atlantic Ocean from flooding their land at high tides. At times, the land is still in danger of flooding. So they build their houses on stilts to protect them from deep water. After the heavy rains (about 140 inches in January) some of the dams of their lakes broke and flooded the land in March 2005. Some of the houses were 3 feet under water, and the residents had to go grocery shopping in boats for about 5 weeks. So they are acquainted with hardships.

The English got many Indians from India to do their work. Guyana was an English Colony until 40 years ago, when they got their Independence. There is much crime in the land. The people have fences around their homes and the gates are locked day and night. Of the 750,000 people of Guyana, about 46% are Indians from India and about 42% are Blacks from Africa.

In 1781, the British forces arrived and forced the Dutch settlement to surrender. The next year, with the help of the French, the Dutch came back and forced the British to surrender. Later, the English won the struggle. In 1812, the area of Kingston in the north was named George Town in honor of the British Prince Regent who later became King George IV. On 21 August 1843 Georgetown was raised to the rank of a city, became the seat of Government, and an office was erected there. Guyana became an independent nation on Thursday, 26 May 1966. Public buildings were brightly decorated with streamers bearing the colors of the Guyana

flag. The Queen Elizabeth Park was renamed the National Park. At midnight, the Union Jack, the symbol of British colonial rule for 163 years, was lowered and the new flag of Guyana was raised to the top of the mast. Just before the flag raising ceremony, Prime Minister Forbes Burnham and Opposition Leader Cheddi Jagan publicly embraced each other. The next morning the Parliament of Guyana met. The portrait of Sir Walter Raleigh, decorating the wall of the Parliament chamber, was removed and replaced with a portrait of Prime Minister Burnham. So the descendents of the slaves and common workers had become the leaders of the nation of Guyana.

Forbes Burnham was a very popular man and was thought to be a great leader for the hour of freedom. He was a lay preacher of the Methodist church. However, his leadership turned sour. Rev. Clayton Rodney expressed it this way, "He had two demons:

witchcraft and communism." He and Castro became buddies, and Burnham became a Dictator. He reigned for 28 years and died in office. There were elections, but they were rigged in his favor. He was Black and the next ruler was Indian. They are struggling now, but with good leadership they can have a good future.

What Is So Wrong About Gambling?

We have many gamblers in our social order today. Regularly a fourth of the general population purchases a lottery ticket during the course of the week—and many claim to be Christians. Some people gamble on ball games, some on slot machines, lotteries, and raffles, and others on poker or some other form of gambling.

Sometime ago, I read an article of a lady airman of the Air Force who had lost thousands of dollars on the gambling machines provided by the BXs. She was in big financial trouble, and she was in the process of suing the Air Force, who made it so easy for her to gamble.

When I was a teenager, I was taught a very important lesson on gambling. One Saturday evening I had a pocket full of nickels. That was about 67 years ago, so nickels had much more spending power than now. It was in Spears Drug Store in Jacksboro, Texas. I encountered that "one armed bandit." I put my money in the slot and pulled the lever, and a lapful of money came out. I was rich for a few minutes. That was so easy that I did it again, and again, and again. But to my surprise, the money well went dry. I remember that my feeling of exultation turned to depression and shame! Before I left that night, I had put every nickel that I could find in that evil machine. That was a very good learning experience for me.

With that experience and the observing of the practice of other gamblers, I have come to the conclusion that gambling has no redemptive value. It is trying to get something from others without any productive work. Gamblers and gambling are not good for the betterment of society. It brings poverty to many families. Time used in gambling is a waste of precious time.

So that night at Spears Drug Store gave me a good lesson in economics and personal responsibility. It was a lesson that I needed to know. The mature life of responsibility is not in lotteries, raffles, and poker, but it is a life of faith, and the mature individual accumulates his wealth by productive means. That person, who lives by honest work, is a blessing to the social structure.

God Told Me So

We have many experiences in life. Some are good, and some are not so good. Some make indelible impressions on our mind, and some are soon forgotten. Job had a time of intensive struggle, and he expressed his desire to have an audience with the Eternal. He had some complaints that he wanted to present before God. Finally, that day came when he had a meeting with the Almighty. The experience was so great and intimidating that he saw himself clearly and repented "in dust and ashes!"

I had an experience with the Almighty that has given me inspiration and direction for many years. It happened 3 August 1976 at noontime, which was 30 years ago. We were having church problems at Emmanuel Baptist Church. The trouble was such that is was beyond my scope of ability to do anything constructive about it. That day I came home to eat, and after the noonday meal, I went to our bedroom to lie down and relax for a few minutes before I returned to the church.

While I was lying down on the bed, I saw a vision of my small Greek New Testament hovering about 3 feet over my head. While gazing upon it, there appeared a rectangular object in the middle of the Greek text. Then there was a bright light that highlighted the words inside the little book. The words were in English and they were: "You are guarded." I rose up and meditated on the words. Then I lay back down. Then the same vision was repeated, except the words had changed. This time the words were: "Read again the glories of the early church."

After that I went to the church and to my office. Mrs. Kay, my secretary, was in the adjoining office. I understood that the meaning of the vision was for me to read again the Book of Acts. So as I sat down and started to read the first verse of Acts, I heard a friendly voice in Mrs. Kay's office. It was Rev. J. B. Scarce, Pastor of Saint Paul's Methodist Church, and he was looking for me.

It was a very productive meeting with eternal implications. He said that he had heard about some of the problems at the church, and he had come to pray for me. It seemed like the Lord had sent him there at that very moment to give me encouragement. It was a meeting I shall never forget. Before he left that day, he suggested that we go to the altar in the Sanctuary and kneel down before the altar and pray. And that is what we did.

For the last 30 years that experience of the visions and the visit with J. B. Scarce has blessed me many times. It was a divine encounter that has colored many, perhaps most, of the decisions that I have made since that blessed day. God leads in many ways. When He communicates with us, it is our responsibility to do His will. That is my objective in life, and I have tried to follow his leading, especially since that day he gave me that two-part vision that will ever be an indelible part of my life.

Why Me Lord?

The question, "Why Me Lord?" has been the thought of people from all cultures around the world. It has plagued the wise men, philosophers, and saints throughout the ages. Books have been written on that subject, and it has been the source of many songs. Many have sought the answer to that profound question. I have also pondered the question.

Why Me Lord? Why did you decide one day just to pick on me? Yes, that question has come up in my mind; so Lord, I would like to ask you a few questions. Questions too profound for we to answer.

Why Me Lord? Why did you pick on me when you gave me a beautiful Christian lady to be me wife for almost 61 years? And Why Me Lord? Why did you pick on me and sent me 4 lovely children to become a part of my life? And Why Me Lord? Why did you send such worthy in-laws to become a part of our Wilton clan? And Why Me Lord, that you should send me six beautiful grandchildren and six beautiful great-grandchildren to continue the blessings of our heritage?

And also, just a word about this Good News of Salvation. Why Me Lord? Why did you pick on me to proclaim it? I had other plans, even to be a big success, but I had no plans or desire to be a preacher. Why did you send me around the world to preach your message, and why did you send me to Japan for 3 years?

Another question. Why Me Lord? Why did you pick on me to have this assignment with Emmanuel Baptist Church for 39 years? Why have you left me here to bask in your sunshine and to enjoy the fellowship of your saints for so many years? Why did you give me so many friends to support me and to pray for me?

And one more question. Why Me Lord? Why is it that your grace is always sufficient when I need it, and why did you give a vision to me when I was groping in darkness?

Really Lord, I have no clue as to why you should have picked on me? So as I ponder the question, Why Me Lord?, I have decided that the answer is not all that important. But thank you Lord for picking on me! The journey has been wonderful and the memories are precious!

LaRue Vivian Haley

It was a great day for me when I left home and went to college, even though I left my mother in tears. I met new friends at Weatherford Junior College, Weatherford, Texas, and I was blessed to be there. My cousin, Herbert Parrish, was a student at North Texas State Teachers College (NTSTC) in Denton, Texas. I wanted to be with him, so I transferred to NTSTC. While I was there my life was changed. After a very traumatic experience, I surrendered to the ministry of Jesus Christ. Then I went back to the farm and lived with my parents for more than a year.

In 1941, I again entered college, and this time it was a Christian school. So I was a student of Howard Payne College in Brownwood, Texas for the next 2 years. It was there that I met LaRue Vivian Haley, who became my wonderful wife for almost 61 years. She came from Hargill,  Texas in south Texas, and I came from Jermyn, Texas, which was in north Texas. We were both working our way through college. I graduated from Howard Payne College in 1943, and we got married 17 October 1943. Aaron, our first-born, arrived in 1945; Fawncyne came in 1952; Kathy arrived in 1955; and Stanley came in 1958.

LaRue was a very devout Christian. While we served in the Air Force, we moved many times. LaRue was always willing to go wherever the assignment directed us to go, whether it was to Hawaii, Japan, or some other assignment. LaRue's mother was also a very wonderful person. Granny Haley was always kind and gracious. When we returned from Hawaii in 1955, Granny Haley was living by herself in a small house in Hargill, Texas. I was assigned to Harlingen Air Force Base in Harlingen, Texas. Then, my next assignment was at Moore Air Base in Mission, Texas. These two Air Force Bases were the only basses in the world that was near Granny Haley. Harlingen Air Force Base was 37 ½ miles east of Hargill, and Moore Air Base was 37 ½ miles west of Granny Haley's house. I will always believe that the orders  for those assignments were directed by someone bigger that the United States Air Force.

LaRue loved the Bible, studied it daily, and lived by its precepts. She was trustworthy in all areas of life. LaRue was a precious mother, a lovely wife, and a loyal friend to her relatives and many others. She was also a faithful steward of her time and money. She had athletic equipment for physical exercises, and she jogged with me for several years.

For the last 23 years of her life, LaRue was plagued with Parkinson's Disease. We went to many doctors and support groups, but she gradually became weaker and weaker. She was critically ill for the last 119 days of her life. At first, she was admitted at St. Joseph's Health Center in Bryan, Texas. Then, she was moved to the Cornerstone Hospital in Austin, Texas. Finally, she was a patient at North Baptist Hospital in San Antonio, Texas.

LaRue told me that she wanted to die at home. It was with the help of Hospice that she lived her last 5 days in her bed at home.

In the last stages, she could only communicate by writing, and sometime it was very difficult to understand her

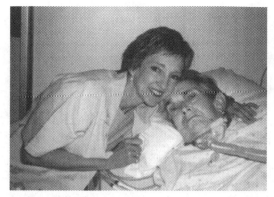

messages. LaRue wrote one day: "Wouldn't it be wonderful if I could wake up someday without Parkinson's Disease?" I agreed that it would, and Faith tells me that her request was honored.

For almost 61 years, I told LaRue that I loved her before we went to sleep at night. I never tired of telling her so, and she never seemed to tire of me telling her of my deep eternal feelings for her. She was truly my "better half."

The Buggy Ride

When I was a young boy, perhaps 5 or 6 years of age, I had an unforgettable experience. Ma (my mother), Grandma Wilton, and I planned a visit to the Parrish family — Aunt Amy, Uncle Jake, Hazel, and Herbert. I was thrilled to think about having a day to play with Herbert. They lived about 4  miles east of us. We would go over the Easter Hill, through the valley, passing by Sam Easter's house, up the next hill by Jim Crum, by the Winn Hill cemetery and the one teacher schoolhouse, and then up another hill near the Bethany Baptist church. Then, we would pass over the hill and down to Uncle Jake's farm. We would have to turn off the road and go through a wire gate and go about a half-mile to his house. So I was thrilled to visualize the trip and a day with Herb.

Grandma had a good buggy, and we had a good mule. I think the mule's name was Old Ider. She would be the power that would pull the buggy. So after hitching Old Ider to the buggy, we were off on the trip. We traveled about a half-mile when we got to the Easter Hill. The hill was very steep and the road turned to the right at the foot of the hill. Grandma Wilton was the driver, and she had the reins in her hand; but, an awful thing happened as we went over the hill.

Old Ider got her tail over the rains and cut off all control from the driver. When Grandma lost control, Old Ider took off down the steep Easter Hill. What a ride that was! It was an experience that I can never forget. At the bottom of the hill there were some deep and wide

bar ditches. The runaway buggy turned over and ended upside down in one of the big bar ditches, which was about three feet deep and three feet wide. The buggy was on top of us, and we were in the ditch. Old Ider had run on down the road and finally stopped in the Easter cotton patch.

After climbing out of the ditch, we started walking up the Easter Hill and back home. Later, some of the men folk retrieved Old Ider and what was left of Grandma and Grandpa's buggy.

The day had begun with a thrill, but we returned home disappointed. However, we were all healthy, with no bone broken, so we had much to be thankful for. We never got to the Parrish farm that day. But we got an experience that shall never be forgotten. As far as I can remember, that was my last buggy ride. But  it really had a good ending, because even though the buggy was broken in many pieces, we all survived without any injury. Praise the Lord for my last buggy ride.

The Hatchery In Ketchikan:
The Salmon Capital Of The World

Terry Sivertsen and I visited a salmon hatchery this morning. In addition to the salmon information, we saw two eagles, an owl, and a sparrow hawk that were injured. They could not be put back into their natural world, because they would not survive. We were told that an eagle has vision that is four times that of 20/20 vision. An eagle could read a newspaper as far away as the length of a football field. An eagle can fly 800 to 900 feet high, and it can see two feet under the water.

In the salmon hatchery there are drawers about 3 feet wide and about 2 feet deep. They were used to hatch out about 100,000 salmon per year. There was also as instrument called a salmon ladder used for the salmon to climb before they were put into the river and eventually released into the sea. It was located in several pools of water about 10 by 10 and about two feet deep. The water went through an exit about two feet to a lower pool. The salmon were put in the lower pool, and they would jump to the higher pool  before they were released from the hatchery.

The hatchery reproduces king salmon and steelhead (sea run rainbow trout). The record for king salmon was 99 pounds. The king salmon is channeled into a holding pen at the hatchery by way of a fish weir that is installed across the stream. This blocks the salmon from going upstream. The weir is made of wire and boards crisscrossed just above the opening to the holding pen. They harvest 35 male and 35 female to extract the eggs and sperm. After the eggs are fertilized, they are put them in trays to incubate. One female king salmon can produce up to 5000 eggs, and the survival rate of the eggs is approximately 70 percent. The incubator that is used at the hatchery is called "the Zinger." It was invented by a friend of the Sivertsen's. It takes two years from the time of fertilization to release into the creek. The fish is called a smolt at the time of release. At one year of age, the fish is called a fingerling, the size of a finger. At 3 months it's called a fry. This is about the size of a minnow. It takes approximately 4 to 5 years from the time of hatching for the salmon to return to the creek to spawn. This occurs in June, the same as steelhead. They come back to the place they were hatched using their ability to discriminate the location by the smell and taste of the water.

The steelhead is a sea run rainbow trout, and it is also produced in this hatchery. Steelhead spawns the same as salmon. They capture 24 males and 24 females using a seine instead of the fish weir, because the steelhead is much smaller and able to pass through the weir. The world record steelhead was caught outside of Ketchikan, weighing 44 pounds. The meat is white and mild in taste. King salmon is usually red but sometime white. The white king salmon is not sold commercially, because people think it should be red. White king salmon is better-tasting than the red, being milder in flavor, according to Terry.

The Misawa Mission Of
The Tokyo Baptist Church

The dedication of the Misawa Baptist Mission of the Tokyo Baptist Church was the fulfillment of a beautiful dream. God works in mysterious ways and His ways are not always Man's ways. He works in the hearts of those who are willing to be led by his spirit—either clergymen or laymen.

The idea of a Baptist Mission in Misawa City, Japan began in the heart of a layman. He talked with many about this work. For many months, he received nothing but discouragement in this endeavor. Many wise men were sought for counsel concerning the establishment of a Baptist Mission in Misawa City, but none thought that it was possible at the time. Bob Nickel was not looking for a dozen reasons why it could not be done, but he was seeking to find a way that it could be done. Thus, he continued to pray and seek for the answer. Finally, others were convinced that it could be done. So in February 1959, five Southern Baptist Military Personnel came together after much prayer and deliberation

 to organize a Baptist mission in Misawa City, Japan. They prayed, they worked, and they planted. By now, they have all rotated back to the states, but the work of the Lord Jesus Christ goes forward. Others came, and they continued the work.

There are now 2 Japanese resident members of the mission. They are taking leadership, and they conduct the worship services and much of the administrative planning. The future of the mission is in their hands. One planted, many watered (1 Cor. 3:6), but God has given the increase.

The number is yet small, but the spirit is great. We shall work together, Japanese and American, to continue and enlarge the work of our Lord Jesus Christ.

Misawa, Japan

One of the hardest things I can remember doing was leaving Harlingen, Texas to go to Misawa, Japan. I had to leave my wife and four children, with the youngest, Stanley, still a baby. I was an Air Force Chaplain, and my orders were for me to report to Misawa Air Base, Japan. As I left early one morning, my thoughts were saddened by having to leave LaRue. I had never heard of Misawa before, and we had been in a war with Japan. I knew no Americans there either. It was a strange feeling; my orders said go, so I went. I drove my car to San Francisco, California; I flew to Misawa air Base, Japan.

In 1955, I had been in Japan for a few days while stationed in Hawaii and on a personal trip through the east. The Chaplain of the Air Force Base where I was visiting in Japan invited me to preach in the Base Chapel. So I was delighted to do so. I do not remember my sermon, but I do remember encouraging the military personnel that day to witness to the Japanese people. They had maids in their homes, and they had many opportunities to witness to them and to others in their workforce about their faith in Jesus.

When I arrived at Misawa Air Base in 1959, I found some military personnel who were obsessed with establishing Christian church in the city of Misawa. The first Sunday that I was there, I was told that a group of airmen were having a Baptist Service in the school building. So I went to the worship service. Baptist hymnals were distributed from a wooden footlocker marked in large bold print, "The First Baptist Church." All the hymnals were stamped with "The First Baptist Church." I was excited to hear about the First Baptist Church in Misawa City. So I asked Sgt. Doyle to tell me where it was. He just smiled and said it is not there yet. What faith! It was not there then, but it is today. However, the name is not "The First Baptist," but its name is "Misawa Baptist Church."

Chaplain Joe Coggins, another Southern Baptist Chaplain, came to Misawa about the same time as I did. Together, we were able to move the Baptist Service to the base chapel. We had our "Baptist Service" each Friday evening. We called it the Baptist service, but we had many who were not Baptist. Our song leader was Ron Williams, a member of the Four Square Church. It was just an informal worship service. We also had special meetings in our homes concerning the Japanese work. The dream of a Baptist church in Misawa was a driving force for many.

Perhaps, the most significant person in establishing Misawa Baptist Church was Junichi Ishikawa (better known  as Johnny), who as the base interpreter for all the chaplains of Misawa Air Base. We became very dear friends. And it was my privilege to baptize him and two others in a public bath. We rented the bath for the service, and others were there for the baptizing service. Johnny became a very zealous disciple of Jesus. He was our connection to the Japanese people. Johnny coordinated the activities between the Christian military personnel and the Japanese Christians—everything from organizing the English classes for the high school students to the purchase of land and the entire church building project.

There was a group of mostly high school students who wanted to learn English. So we rented a room in Misawa City and began to teach. Their desire was to learn English, and our desire was to introduce them to Jesus. So our text was the Gospel of Matthew. A1C Ronald Williams, our song leader in church services, was very instrumental in helping to nurture this class to become a witnessing class. He had great ability to sing and relate to the Japanese young people. Johnny, all during this time, acted as interpreter.

Another key person was Hiroshi Suzuki. He had been listening to the "Voice of America" on the radio waves. He wanted to be with some natives of America who spoke English. So he wrote a letter to the General of Misawa Air Base requesting the opportunity to be in the home of an American family. The General asked the Base Chaplain if any of the chaplains would like to take this young man for the summer. The Staff Chaplain asked me if I would be interested. So I told him that I would check with LaRue to see if we would be interested. LaRue said O.K., so I told the Staff Chaplain we would be glad to take him. That was the beginning of a wonderful relationship between Hero (that was his nickname) and the Wilton family.

We had a wonderful time with Hero. He had good manners and Japanese politeness. I have always liked  buttermilk, so we usually had buttermilk to drink. Hero was greatly relieved when he found out that it was not necessary for him to drink buttermilk. Hero wanted to learn English, but he was also ready to teach Japanese to anyone who was interested in learning to speak Japanese. So we learned many things from Hero. He taught us many things about Japan. He was delighted to do anything we needed for him to do.

Hero was interested in learning English, and I was interested in introducing him to Jesus. So I had the perfect project. I was teaching the book of Matthew to the Japanese young people and Johnny was interpreting, but it would be better if we had the text in Japanese. So that was the job for Hero. He translated the Gospel of Matthew from English to

Japanese. Hero did a great job, and we all had great fellowship.

The time came when we needed to think about a building and the future of the Japanese mission. We needed some Japanese Baptist church to sponsor this mission. There were not many Japanese churches in Japan at that time. However, encouragement was given by Don Heiss and family, who were missionaries in Amori, and Hannah Barlow, who was a missionary in Hakodate. We had many good times with them. It was finally through contact with Milton DuPriest, the pastor of Tokyo Baptist Church, that church support was established for the mission. Although the distance from to Tokyo to Misawa was then about an 8 hour travel by train, it was working through the pastor and the church of the Tokyo Baptist Church that the mission became the Misawa Baptist Mission of the Tokyo Baptist Church. Later, the mission became Misawa Baptist Church. Today, there are actually two churches in Misawa City that have resulted from the Misawa Baptist Mission. There is the Misawa Baptist Church, which ministers to the Japanese people, and there is also the Calvary Baptist Church, which ministers to English speaking people.

Johnny became a lay preacher, and he later made a preaching tour in the USA. He came and preached to our church at the time, the Skyline Baptist Church, located in Killeen, Texas. He sent me money to visit Japan several years later. Fawncyne, our older daughter, and I visited Johnny, who was then in Tokyo. From there, we visited Rev. and Mrs. Kokubo in Tajiri, Miyagi, Japan. We also went to Misawa City and attended a Sunday worship service at the Misawa Baptist Church.

Later, Hero became a Christian, and he came to Texas. He wanted me to baptize him, and I had the privilege of baptizing him into the fellowship of Skyline Baptist Church. For awhile, he was a student at Howard Payne University, and he later went to New York and became the pastor of a Japanese church located in New York. He is now a Christian counselor. At one point, he went back to Japan to get a wife, and they have a daughter, Hanako, who has made many awards in the school that she attends. Hanako was listed in Who's Who Among American High School Students. Hero is now a Christian counselor in New York. His friendship has been a blessing to me over the years, and we still keep in contact. Japan is a great nation with lovely people. It was great to serve in the USAF, endorsed by the Southern Baptist Convention, with the privilege of ministering to the military personnel and making friends with many Japanese people. Thank-you Lord for being so good to me!

India

There are many interesting things about India, and there are many interesting places to see in India. It is the second largest nation in the world. It has gone through many political systems. It has had good times and bad times. The Moguls, from Mongolia, conquered India in 1526 and founded a Muslim empire that lasted until the nineteenth century. Later, the British conquered India, and it was under the British rule for many years. However, today India is ruled by its own people.

It was my privilege to be in India two times. The first time was in 1955 while I was an Air Force Chaplain at Wheeler Air Base in Hawaii. At that time, I was on an educational tour of the Holy Land, flying space-available on Air Force planes. Originally, I was scheduled for a three-day stop at Delhi, India. However, due to mechanical problems, our flight was grounded, and since only one plane a week came through Delhi, my tour in India was extended to 10 days. Years later, my second trip to India was while I was the pastor of Emmanuel Baptist Church in Bryan, Texas. On that occasion, I went to Ajmere, India for a Christian crusade, and that also lasted about 10 days. I have precious memories of those 20 days in India.

The visit to the Taj Mahal was, indeed, a wonderful experience. The Taj Mahal represents a great love story. It is one of the wonders of the world and the pride and glory of Indian architecture. It is a mausoleum dedicated to Mumtaz Mahal by Shah Jahan, who was the Master of India.

Mumtaz Mahal married Shah Jahan when she was 21 years of age. "For 18 years, until her death in 1631 A.D., she

was the emperor's trusted companion and the married life was one of perfect harmony" (Agra, Tourist Association of India, p.5). She bore 14 children, and she died immediately after the birth of their last child. Shah Jahan was filled with grief and lived as a mendicant for the next 2 years. It was during this time that he envisioned the building the Taj Mahal. Shah Jahan invited to his court the eminent architects, masons, and artists from the Mogul Empire, and those also from Iran, Turkey, and Arabia. It took about 20,000 men to build this monument. The tomb stands on a marble platform that is 22 feet high, and the tomb itself is some 186 square feet and 243 feet tall.

Shah Jahan planned to build another mausoleum on the other side of the Jamuna River, but it never happened. Aurangzeb, his son, usurped the throne and imprisoned the

old and ailing emperor in Agra Fort. There was a large concave lens in the fort from which he could see the Taj Mahal by looking through it. Aurangzeb killed his 12 brothers and built beautiful mausoleums for

all of them. When Shah Jahan died in 1666 A.D., he was buried beside is wife in the Taj Mahal.

It was my privilege to visit both the Taj Mahal and Agra Fort. They were, indeed, wonderful sights to behold. At the tomb of Mumtaz Mahal, the guide pointed out that the stone that was at the head of the coffin was taken by the British, and it is now in the Queen of England's Royal Crown. At Agra Fort, the guide pointed out how the old deposed emperor could look through the lenses to see across the Jamuna River and see the Taj Mahal.

When I went to Ajmere, Rajasthan for a Christian crusade, Rev. S.K. Paul was my interpreter and provider for a week. When I got off the train in the city of Ajmere, I waited for a few minutes at the train station. While I was waiting, a pitiful woman with a little baby in her arms came to me for a handout. I really did not have much money, but I gave her a coin. Then, another woman with a little baby appeared for a

handout. I told Rev. Paul about it, and he said, "If you had given her money, a third one would have appeared." We had a great time with the church, and one day we took a trip to see some of the glories of Northern India. And I shall always remember riding an elephant. Bro. Paul was a great musician. His ambition was to get the Gospel Message to the 27,000 villages of Rajasthan. As I was leaving on the train, Rev. Paul, walking by my window of the moving train, told me that he needed an accordion for his Gospel ministry. After I returned home, the Emmanuel Baptist Church and I sent him an accordion. He was filled with gratitude, and he sent us pictures of his work. He had a great ministry in Northern India.

At Delhi, India is the tomb of Mahatma Gandhi. He was one of the greatest of the leaders of men. He was unselfish and wanted and worked for the people of India to have freedom. It was through his leadership that India did receive her freedom.  His memorial was very simple, but his life, compared with the life of Shah Jahan, was greater as light is over darkness. The brilliance of his influence will shine upon India for many years. India has many good people today. My Indian friends have blessed me greatly, and I have many fond memories of my visits to India.

Emmanuel Lighthouse Mission

Emmanuel Lighthouse Mission began about 35 years ago as a part of Emmanuel Baptist Church. Originally, there were two Bryan Air Force barracks buildings on church property across the street from the church sanctuary and educational building. For a time, one of the buildings was used as a Coffee House for the young people of Emmanuel Baptist Church, and the other building was used for Sunday school rooms. However, both buildings were idle when Dayton Phillips came to become a member of the church. Dayton had been on drugs, and he needed a place to live to be away from those who were involved in drugs. He received money each month from oil wells on his estate.

Dayton was given permission to live in one of the buildings. So, with carpenter tools and his carpentry skills, Dayton tore down walls and erected others converted one of the buildings into living quarters. That  became his home for a few years. Dayton was a very productive member of the church, and he later became a gospel minister and one of the pastors of Emmanuel Baptist Church. Aaron Wilton also moved to Bryan and bought a house near the church. He became one of the deacons of the church and had a leading role in the development of the mission work.

About that time, there was a great need by refugees of many foreign countries to have a home. So, for several years, Emmanuel Baptist Church became the home for many refugees. Some came from Viet Nam, some from China, some from Cuba, and some from other places in the Orient. The greatest number came from Laos.

The Saeterns and the Saechaos were such Christian families, and they became a great blessing to the church. Rev. Dayton Phillips married Nai Meng Saetern, who was from Laos. Kao Meng Saetern and Nai Seng Saechao became ministers of the Gospel, and they are today serving their people in California and their homeland.

At one time, we used one of spare buildings for men and the other for women. However, that did not work out very well. After 2 or 3 of the women became pregnant, we decided that we could not accommodate both men and women. We then decided to use the buildings to shelter homeless women and children. Many women and children came, and at one time we had as many as 36 women and children. We began having no pantry and no rules. If they were hungry, we provided them with beans and rice. Many would stay up late at night and then sleep most of the next morning. We saw that we had problems. We put smoke detectors in the building, but some of the batteries ended up in a radio. So, we decided to make some rules, such as setting a curfew, requiring them to get a job, to attend church, to work in the church garden on Saturday mornings, etc.

So, the ministry of the Women's shelter has evolved. Dayton came up with the name,

Emmanuel Lighthouse Mission, and we tagged it ELM. We had some wonderful ladies who were directors of the Women's shelter: Melissa Freeman, Noelle McNabb, and Marian Cune. They were great leaders who have caused the ELM to be what it is today. We seek to share Jesus with those who come our way. We believe that God's grace is sufficient for those who are in need. God has given us a love for all who come to stay with us, and we pray that the time with us will be an eternal blessing to them.

The Garden

I grew up on a farm, and we always had a garden. My mother was a great gardener. We had beans, English peas, black-eyed peas, onions, collard greens, beets, and many other vegetables. We also had a variety of weeds that came up among the good vegetables. When the ground was wet, the weeds could be easily pulled up. My mother often sent me to the garden to pull weeds. That was a job I never liked.

We always had plenty to eat, even during the Depression Years. Uncle Bob, my mother's brother whose name was Wylie Durgan Rhoades, lived with us during those days. We usually had plenty of Black-eyed peas and other vegetables to eat. I remember that our favorite delicacy was buttermilk with cornbread and onions. I still remember Uncle Bob with his big bowl of buttermilk and cornbread, and that was a full meal with no complaints. That was a banquet to remember!

The Bible tells us about three gardens: the Garden of Eden, the Garden of Gethsemane, and the Garden of Paradise. Adam & Eve were put in the Garden of Eden to care for it. Jesus prayed in the Garden of Gethsemane. The Garden of Paradise is the future home for God's people. So the garden is a very important place.

For many years, Emmanuel Baptist Church has had a garden. The ladies who live in the Women's Shelter work in the garden on Saturday mornings, unless they have jobs that interfere with that work. We have given other people in the community the opportunity to use a plot for their own

 gardens, and we have had some who have taken a part the in garden work. Beulah Brown, a neighbor nearby, was one of our best gardeners. One year, she had more broccoli than we needed, and she had other vegetables to go with it. We have had bumper crops of tomatoes, sugar snap peas, okra, and other vegetables. Some vegetables like cold weather, and other vegetables like hot weather. So, we can plant seeds throughout the year; however, we usually focus in the Spring garden and the Fall garden.

It is exciting to see things grow, especially those things that we can eat. We put the seed in the ground, and God causes it to grow. It can be a fun time, and the exercise is very good therapy for the body!

Picture Credits

Page *Subject*

Page	Subject
4	My Window On The World (Wilton Family Photo)
7	LaRue Vivian Haley Wilton (Wilton Family Photo)
8	Verda Lee & Wanda Crum (Crum Family photo)
8	Maryanne Rivers (Wilton Family Photo)
13	The Sphinx (Wilton Family Photo)
15	"Pa" (Elmer Elisha Wilton; Wilton Family Photo)
16	Farm wagon (Wilton Family photo)
18	Farm wagon (Wilton Family photo)
19	Baby goats (Internet Composite)
20	Pocket watch (Internet Composite)
20	Clock face (Internet Composite)
26	Jacksboro, Texas Town Square
27	Lewis Baker/Winn Hill tabernacle (Wilton Photo)
28	Church organ console (Internet Composite)
30	Winn Hill schoolhouse c.1929 (Wilton Family Photo)
32	Van & Anthony Wilton (Wilton Family Photo)
34	Windmill (Internet Composite)
35	Winn Hill, Texas (Wilton Family Photo)
36	Clyde Wilton/Misawa, Japan (Wilton Family Photo)
38	H.F. & Martha Wilton (Wilton Family Photo)
39	Winn Hill, Texas (Wilton Family Photo)
40	H.F. & Martha Wilton (Wilton Family Photo)
41	Kids on Model T (Internet Composite)
46	Clyde Wilton & Atwood Reynolds (Wilton Photo)
47	Hand-cranked Wall Telephone (Internet Composite)
49	Bathhouse Baptism/Japan (Wilton Family Photo)
51	Larue Wilton & Friend (Wilton Family Photo)
54	Stack of Bibles (Internet Composite)
59	Fawncyne & Kathy Wilton/Japan (Wilton Photo)
62	Clyde Wilton & Herbert Parrish (Wilton Photo)
64	Socrates bust (Internet Composite)

Page *Subject*

66   Taj Mahal, India (Wilton Family Photo)
67   Clyde at Empty Tomb/Israel (Wilton Family Photo)
69   Clyde & Larue Wilton at EBC (Wilton Family Photo)
70   Larue & Clyde Wilton at home (Wilton Photo)
71   Military color guard (Internet Composite)
72   Aaron Wilton at airport (Wilton Family Photo)
74   Robert Worley & Clyde Wilton (Wilton Photo)
76   Clyde Wilton Family (Wilton Family Photo)
77   Tommy Chapman on horse (Family Photo)
77   Bennett & Ashton Syptak (Wilton Family Photo)
78   Braden, Ethan, Connor Buche (Wilton Family Photo)
79   Elmer & Eula Wilton (Wilton Family Photo)
80   Larue & Clyde Wilton (Wilton Family Photo)
85   Aaron Wilton at airport (Wilton Family Photo)
87   Japanese-style meal (Wilton Family Photo)
89   Clyde & Family at Checkers (Wilton Family Photo)
90   Clyde & Family at Dominoes (Wilton Family Photo)
90   Clyde with grandchildren (Wilton Family Photo)
92   Leaning Tower of Pisa (Internet Composite)
95   Jerusalem hillside (Wilton Family Photo)
97   Misawa Baptist Church, Japan (Wilton Photo)
98   Clyde & Larue 50th Anniversary (Wilton Photo)
102 Bryan Lake Baptism (Wilton Family Photo)
106 Harvester in pasture (Internet Composite)
114 Barbed wire fence (Internet Composite)
116 Winn Hill church construction (Wilton Photo)
118 Family Feeding Cattle (Wilton Family Photo)
120 Larue & Fawncyne Wilton/Hawaii (Wilton Photo)
127 Crum at 4H function (Crum Family Photo)
131 Razor with strop (Internet Composite)
147 Jacksboro, Texas Town Square
150 Honeybee hives (Wilton Family Photo)
151 Clyde Wilton in pulpit (Wilton Family Photo)

Page   _Subject_

151   Lety & Patrick Johnson (Wilton Family Photo)
152   Bryan Lake Baptism singing (Wilton Family Photo)
152   Clyde Wilton & Tom Baber (Wilton Family Photo)
153   Bryan Lake Baptism (Wilton Family Photo)
156   Jerusalem ruins (Wilton Family Photo)
162   Jim Crum & wife (Crum Family Photo)
162   Crum cousins (Crum Family Photo)
164   Crum Family (Crum Family Photo)
169   Crum Family (Crum Family Photo)
170   Bethany Baptist Church painting (Wilton Photo)
170   Church in Hawaii (Wilton Family Photo)
171   Clyde Wilton at EBC (Wilton Family Photo)
173   Butterfly on Flower (Wilton Family Photo)
176   Jermyn High School (Wilton Family Photo)
177   Jermyn High School (Wilton Family Photo)
178   Larue Vivian Haley Wilton (Wilton Family Photo)
179   Robert & Fawncyne Worley (Wilton Family Photo)
181   Clyde & group with Salmon (Wilton Family Photo)
181   Clyde Wilton in Alaska (Wilton Family Photo)
183   Clyde beside seaplane/Alaska (Wilton Photo)
185   Clyde & group in Alaska (Wilton Family Photo)
186   Church in Guyana (Wilton Family Photo)
187   University Of Guyana sign (Wilton Family Photo)
187   Inside Guyana church (Wilton Family Photo)
188   Steven Babalola in Guyana (Wilton Family Photo)
194   Clyde Wilton in garden (Wilton Family Photo)
195   Children of Clyde Wilton (Wilton Family Photo)
196   Eula Wilton & Marintha Haley (Wilton Photo)
197   Fawncyne Worley & Larue Wilton (Wilton Photo)
198   Flowers in Field (Wilton Family Photo)
198   Hillside Road (Wilton Family Photo)
199   Horse-drawn buggy (Internet Composite)
200   Clyde Wilton driving boat (Wilton Family Photo)

Page	Subject
202	Clyde at Misawa Baptist Mission (Wilton Photo)
203	Misawa Air Base, Japan sign (Wilton Family Photo)
205	Misawa Baptist Church, Japan (Wilton Photo)
206	Clyde Wilton & Hiroshi Suzuki (Wilton Photo)
208	Japanese lake baptism (Wilton Family Photo)
209	Train Station in India (Wilton Family Photo)
210	Taj Mahal from the air (Wilton Family Photo)
210	Agra Fort from the air (Wilton Family Photo)
211	Downtown in India (Wilton Family Photo)
212	Bathing in Ganges River (Wilton Family Photo)
213	Dayton Phillips & Patrick Johnson (Wilton Photo)
214	Saetern Family (Saetern Family Photo)
214	Sister Mary in ELM garden (Wilton Family Photo)
215	Saetern celebration (Saetern Family Photo)
216	Clyde Wilton in ELM garden (Wilton Family Photo)
217	Beulah Brown in ELM garden (Wilton Photo)
217	ELM Residents in garden (Wilton Family Photo)